Curriculum Map

Course	Level 1	Level 2	Level 3	Level 4	Level 5	Level 6	Level 7	Text Book
General Conversation	Essential English : Begin Again / Pre Get Up to Speed 1~2 / Daily Focused English 1	New Get Up to Speed 1 / Daily Focused English 2	New Get Up to Speed 2	New Get Up to Speed 3	New Get Up to Speed 4			
Discussion			Active Discussion 1	Active Discussion 1 / Active Discussion 2 / Chicken Soup Course	Active Discussion 2 / Dynamic Discussion / Chicken Soup Course / Dynamic Information & Digital Technology	Dynamic Discussion / Dynamic Information & Digital Technology	Dynamic Discussion	
Business Conversation	Pre Business Basics 1	Pre Business Basics 2	Pre Business Basics 2 / Business Basics 1	Business Basics 1 / Business Basics 2	Business Basics 2 / Business Practice 1	Business Practice 1 / Business Practice 2	Business Practice 2	
Global Biz Workshop				Effective Business Writing Skills (Workbook) / Effective Presentation Skills (Workbook)	Effective Business Writing Skills (Workbook) / Effective Presentation Skills (Workbook) / Effective Negotiation Skills (Workbook) / Cross-Cultural Training 1~2 (Workbook) / Leadership Training Course (Workbook)	Effective Negotiation Skills (Workbook) / Cross-Cultural Training 1~2 (Workbook) / Leadership Training Course (Workbook)		
Business Skills				Simple & Clear Technical Writing Skills / Effective Business Writing Skills / Effective Meeting Skills / Business Communication (Negotiation) / Effective Presentation Skills	Effective Business Writing Skills / Effective Meeting Skills / Business Communication (Negotiation) / Effective Presentation Skills / Marketing 1	Marketing 1 / Marketing 2 / Management	Marketing 2 / Management	
On the Job English			Construction English in Use 1~4 / Public Service English in Use	Construction English in Use 1~4 / Public Service English in Use	Human Resources / Accounting and Finance / Marketing and Sales / Production Management / Automotive / Banking and Commerce / Medical and Medicine / Information Technology / Construction	Human Resources / Accounting and Finance / Marketing and Sales / Production Management / Automotive / Banking and Commerce / Medical and Medicine / Information Technology / Construction		

※ This Curriculum Map illustrates the entire line-up of textbooks at CARROT HOUSE.

Pre Business Basics 2

Introduction

Carrot House Methodology

Andragogical Approach & Productive English

The teaching of children (pedagogy) and adult learning (andragogy) are distinctively different. Pedagogy is akin to training and encourages convergent thinking and rote learning. It is compulsory, centered on the teacher and the imparting of information with minimal control by the learner. Andragogy, by contrast, is about education as freedom. It encourages divergent thinking and active learning. It is voluntary, learner oriented, and opens up vistas for continuing learning. Adults need to feel independent and in control of their learning. Therefore, Carrot House curriculum is based on andragogy and is designed to encourage learners' participation and engagement by providing more task-based activities and opportunities to frequently interact in the classroom.

People want to achieve communicative competence when they learn other languages. English education in EFL environments has been rather focused on the receptive skills of English—listening and reading—which simply increases learners' knowledge about a language, not the competence of using it. If people are well equipped with productive skills—speaking and writing—they will be competent in English communication.

This is why Carrot House curriculum is designed to enhance learners' productive skills throughout the course. This andragogical approach of the Carrot House Curriculum, which focuses on productive English, will enable learners to achieve communication skills necessary for global competence. Carrot House's teaching philosophy and curriculum combine to provide a "Language for Success" for all learners.

Communicative Language Learning (CLL)

This communicative interaction, the essential component of language acquisition, does not occur in a typical, non-meaningful, fun-oriented conversation with native speakers. It occurs in a negotiated interaction through which a well-trained teacher provides the comprehensible input that is appropriate to the learners. The learners, at the same time, actively utilize the opportunities given to them by the teachers.

To this end, the Communicative Language Learning (CLL) method is employed in the field of Foreign Language Acquisition. The CLL method provides activities that are geared toward using language pragmatically, authentically, and functionally with the intention of achieving meaningful purposes.

Course Overview

Objectives

The Pre Business Basics Series is designed as an introduction to the Business Basics and Business Practice textbooks. The textbooks are targeted at beginner level learners and aims to enhance their communication skills in the workplace. The wide range of situations given in each book allows learners to establish skills not only in business communication but also develop grammar, listening and comprehension skills. Through constant classroom interactions, learners can improve their proficiency and gain confidence in international business transactions.

PRE
BUSINESS
BASICS

- Getting Started
- Language Preview
- The Formal Sort
- Interactions
- Attentive Listening
- Business Basics
- Talking Shop
- Case Study

2

CARROT HOUSE
P.O.Box #2924, St. Marys, Ontario, Canada

Pre Business Basics 2
© Carrot House

All rights reserved. No part of this publication may be reproduced, stored in a retrieval system, or transmitted in any form or by any means without the prior permission in writing of Carrot House

Printed : July 2019

Author : Carrot Language Lab

ISBN 978-89-6732-139-0

Printed and distributed in Korea
9F, 488, Gangnam St., Gangnam-gu, Seoul 06120, Korea

Lesson Composition

Pre Business Basics 2 consists of 10 lessons and 5 review activities. Each lesson consists of 8 sections.

1. Getting Started

This two part activity is designed to stimulate the learner's thinking through simple, situation-related questions and expression questions with visual prompts.

Good To Know

This activity provides learners with a chance to review mistakes frequently made by EFL learners. Answers and explanations are provided in the appendix at the back of the book.

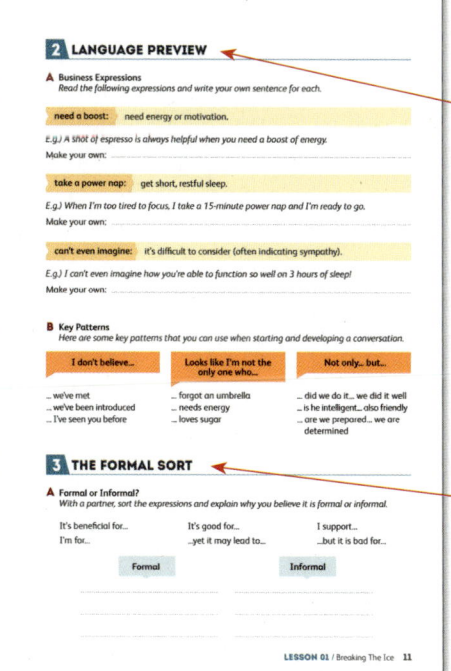

2. Language Preview

Preview selected vocabulary terms and language patterns that will be used throughout the lesson and practice the business expressions given in part A, and the patterns through substitution drills in part B.

3. The Formal Sort

Sort commonly used expressions into formal and informal categories. Use the expressions throughout the lesson for understanding the language differences in formal and casual communication. The answers are provided in the appendix at the back of the book.

Pre Business Basics 2

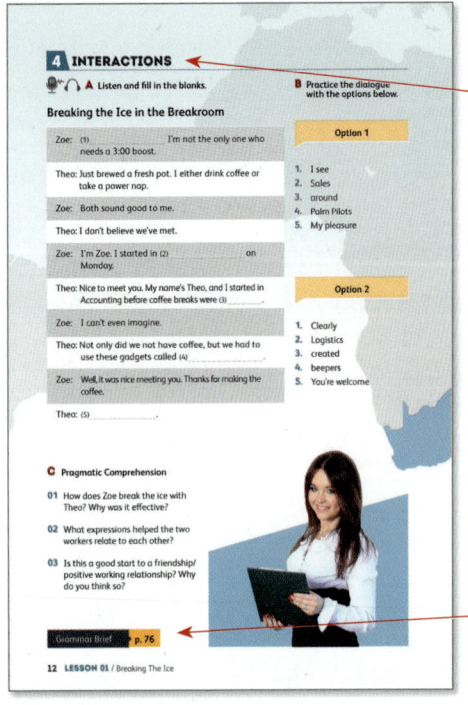

4. Interactions

Understand the mission of each business character and role play to practice English speaking in business situations. Help learners improve their comprehension skills and utilize key language patterns. Use the three part activity to practice listening, speaking, and comprehension. Speaking Training along with mp3 files are available via e-book, and audio scripts are provided in the appendix at the back of the book.

Grammar Brief

Additional grammar explanations and practice activities are provided in the appendix at the back of the book.

5. Attentive Listening

Extended dialogues and questions help provide a balanced set of communication skills, in particular, receptive skills. Active listening activities including true or false, fill in the blanks, and matching activities provide learners with an opportunity to expand on their listening and comprehension skills. Mp3 files are available via e-book, and audio scripts are provided in the appendix at the back of the book.

Quote of the Day

Provides open ended discussion topics through reflecting on popular and famous quotes.

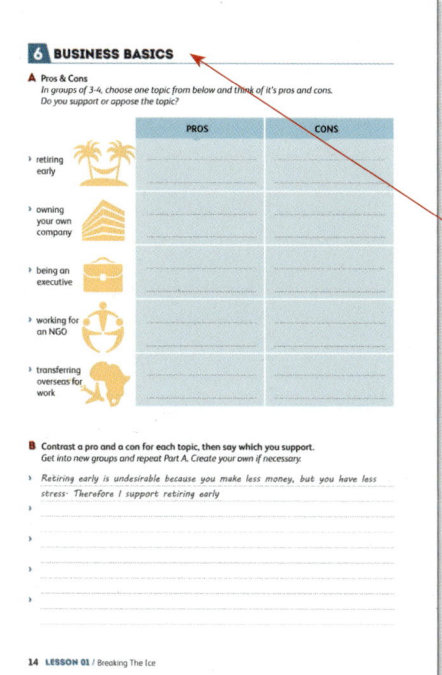

6. Business Basics

Expand learners' ability to develop essential business skills with English as the medium. Language terms and grammar from each lesson can be utilized in a practical business setting.

7. Talking Shop

Topically guided questions encourage learners to discuss concepts from each lesson. Learners can practice speaking freely, offering their opinions, and explore a variety of situations within a given topic.

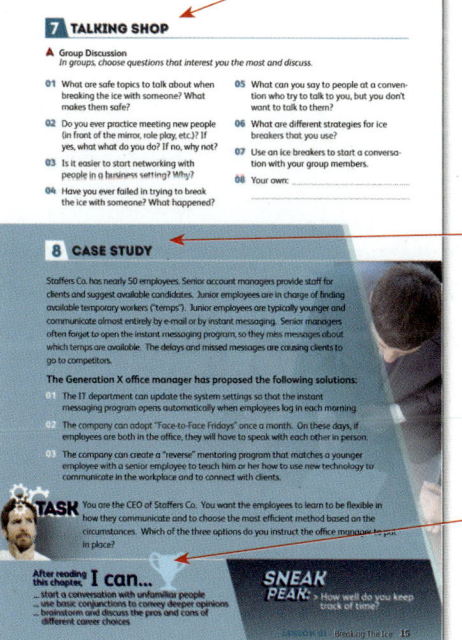

8. Case Study

This section puts learners' business knowledge, thinking, and language skills to the test. Learners' can discuss possible solutions and outcomes to given business case scenarios based on actual events.

Review and Sneak Peek

Provides learners with an area to reflect on the language and skills learned in the lesson and glimpse into the topic to be studied next.

CONTENTS

Unit.01

Lesson Title	Learning Objectives	Language Practice	Business Basics	Page
Lesson.01 **Breaking The Ice**	- start a conversation with unfamiliar people - use basic conjunctions to convey deeper opinions - brainstorm and discuss the pros and cons of different career choices	· I don't believe… · Looks like I'm not the only one who… · Not only… but…	Pros & Cons	10
Lesson.02 **It's Time!**	- schedule time to meet someone - use hour-first and minute-first time expressions to schedule meetings - meet a co-worker after work	· I'm free… · I'm off by… · Let's say…	Meeting After Working	16
		» Review 01		

Unit.02

Lesson Title	Learning Objectives	Language Practice	Business Basics	Page
Lesson.03 **Navigating Your Area**	- identify common places and features in an office building - use prepositions to provide directions - give directions to areas in an office	· Where might I find…? · It's… down… · It's right…	Giving Directions	23
Lesson.04 **Trending Topics**	- communicate basic trends on a graph - use simple past, present perfect, and dummy subjects for market analysis - explain a line graph	· … hit a peak of… · This… tells us… · As you can see…	Companies in Contrast	29
		» Review 02		

Unit.03

Lesson Title	Learning Objectives	Language Practice	Business Basics	Page
Lesson.05 **Everything You Want**	- talk about wants, hopes, and dreams - use present perfect continuous to communicate desires and goals - explain your goals on a timeline	· My dream is to… · I've been wanting to… · Keep… and I'll keep…	Timeline of Desires	36
Lesson.06 **What Happened?**	- explain a past action that was interrupted - use simple past with past continuous to explain two concurrent past actions - complete and explain a product problem form	· I was… when… · I tried… but… · Could you… when you're done?	Product Problem Return Form	42
		» Review 03		

Unit.04

Lesson Title	Learning Objectives	Language Practice	Business Basics	Page
Lesson.07 **Getting Some Help**	- ask for help - use politeness strategies to make requests - politely ask for help or deny help if unable to provide it	· Would you mind...? · I need you to... · You might want to...	Help List	49
Lesson.08 **Proper Conduct**	- identify common Western etiquette practices - use type 2 conditionals to give advice - recognize and discuss acceptable manners while dining	· If someone... do the same. · I'll be sure to... · I've got to say...	Dining Etiquette	55
	» Review 04			

Unit.05

Lesson Title	Learning Objectives	Language Practice	Business Basics	Page
Lesson.09 **Sorry For That**	- apologize for causing an inconvenience - use sequence words to organize your ideas - assess apologies for effectiveness	· I could use your help with... · It looks like I... · He's great with...	Corporate Apologies	62
Lesson.10 **Saying Goodbye**	- say goodbye after a business trip - use passive tense to communicate your thoughts about people and accomplishments - send a farewell e-mail to a colleague	· If you're ever... let me know. · I genuinely appreciate... · Give my best to...	Saying Farewell	68
	» Review 05			

Index

Appendix	Page
Grammar Brief	76
Audio Scripts	86
Common Mistakes (Answer Key)	91
The Formal Sort (Answer Key)	95

LESSON
01
BREAKING THE ICE

OBJECTIVES

After this chapter, you will be able to...

- start a conversation with unfamiliar people
- use basic conjunctions to convey deeper opinions
- brainstorm and discuss the pros and cons of different career choices

1 GETTING STARTED

A Let's look at the image.
Describe what's happening in the picture.

Why are moments like these so important in office environments?

B Discuss the questions below:

> What's a good way to get people smiling or laughing in your culture? Why doesn't it happen more often?

> What are helpful ways to break the ice with someone?

> Is it easier or harder to break the ice with someone from another culture? Why?

One or both? *Circle the best answer. Check your answers in the back of the book.*

> I bought him a present. I did it **to / for** him.
> Apples are good **to / for** you.
> My co-worker is good **to / for** me.

2 LANGUAGE PREVIEW

A Business Expressions
Read the following expressions and write your own sentence for each.

need a boost: need energy or motivation.

E.g.) A shot of espresso is always helpful when you need a boost of energy.
Make your own: _____

take a power nap: get short, restful sleep.

E.g.) When I'm too tired to focus, I take a 15-minute power nap and I'm ready to go.
Make your own: _____

can't even imagine: it's difficult to consider (often indicating sympathy).

E.g.) I can't even imagine how you're able to function so well on 3 hours of sleep!
Make your own: _____

B Key Patterns
Here are some key patterns that you can use when starting and developing a conversation.

I don't believe...	Looks like I'm not the only one who...	Not only... but...
... we've met	... forgot an umbrella	... did we do it... we did it well
... we've been introduced	... needs energy	... is he intelligent... also friendly
... I've seen you before	... loves sugar	... are we prepared... we are determined

3 THE FORMAL SORT

A Formal or Informal?
With a partner, sort the expressions and explain why you believe it is formal or informal.

It's beneficial for...   It's good for...   I support...
I'm for...   ...yet it may lead to... ...but it is bad for...

Formal	Informal

LESSON 01 / Breaking The Ice

4 INTERACTIONS

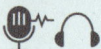 **A** Listen and fill in the blanks.

B Practice the dialogue with the options below.

Breaking the Ice in the Breakroom

Zoe: (1) _____ I'm not the only one who needs a 3:00 boost.

Theo: Just brewed a fresh pot. I either drink coffee or take a power nap.

Zoe: Both sound good to me.

Theo: I don't believe we've met.

Zoe: I'm Zoe. I started in (2) _____ on Monday.

Theo: Nice to meet you. My name's Theo, and I started in Accounting before coffee breaks were (3) _____.

Zoe: I can't even imagine.

Theo: Not only did we not have coffee, but we had to use these gadgets called (4) _____.

Zoe: Well, it was nice meeting you. Thanks for making the coffee.

Theo: (5) _____.

Option 1
1. I see
2. Sales
3. around
4. Palm Pilots
5. My pleasure

Option 2
1. Clearly
2. Logistics
3. created
4. beepers
5. You're welcome

C Pragmatic Comprehension

01 How does Zoe break the ice with Theo? Why was it effective?

02 What expressions helped the two workers relate to each other?

03 Is this a good start to a friendship/positive working relationship? Why do you think so?

Grammar Brief p. 76

5 ATTENTIVE LISTENING

🎧 **Extended Dialogue** · *Three co-workers talk near an exit at work as they wait for the weather to improve.*

A Active Listening. Think about the following questions as you listen. Write the answers in the spaces below.

› How does Zoe break the ice? ....

› What do the co-workers talk about? ....

› What information do we discover about the co-workers? ....

B True or False. Circle T for true and F for false. Explain your answer.

01 No one brought an umbrella to work.   T /(F)   *"False! Dan brought an umbrella but left it in the car."*

02 Zoe thinks waiting is not any fun.   T / F   ....

03 One of the workers believes he is not very intelligent.   T / F   ....

04 Zoe thinks Miami is the worst place to live.   T / F   ....

05 Zoe and Steve have seen each other before.   T / F   ....

Audio Script   p. 86

QUOTE OF THE DAY

A man and a friend are playing golf one day at their local golf course. One of the guys is about to chip his ball onto the green when he sees funeral cars next to the course. He stops in mid-swing, takes off his golf cap, closes his eyes, and bows down in prayer. His friend says: "Wow, that is the most thoughtful and touching thing I have ever seen. You truly are a kind man." The man then replies: "Yeah, well we were married 35 years."

› What made this joke funny or not so funny?

› Do jokes make good icebreakers? Why do you think so?

LESSON 01 / Breaking The Ice

6. BUSINESS BASICS

A Pros & Cons
In groups of 3-4, choose one topic from below and think of it's pros and cons. Do you support or oppose the topic?

	PROS	CONS
retiring early		
owning your own company		
being an executive		
working for an NGO		
transferring overseas for work		

B Contrast a pro and a con for each topic, then say which you support.
Get into new groups and repeat Part A. Create your own if necessary.

› *Retiring early is undesirable because you make less money, but you have less stress. Therefore I support retiring early*
›
›
›
›

14 LESSON 01 / Breaking The Ice

7 TALKING SHOP

A Group Discussion
In groups, choose questions that interest you the most and discuss.

01 What are safe topics to talk about when breaking the ice with someone? What makes them safe?

02 Do you ever practice meeting new people (in front of the mirror, role play, etc.)? If yes, what what do you do? If no, why not?

03 Is it easier to start networking with people in a business setting? Why?

04 Have you ever failed in trying to break the ice with someone? What happened?

05 What can you say to people at a convention who try to talk to you, but you don't want to talk to them?

06 What are different strategies for ice breakers that you use?

07 Use an ice breakers to start a conversation with your group members.

08 Your own: _____

8 CASE STUDY

Staffers Co. has nearly 50 employees. Senior account managers provide staff for clients and suggest available candidates. Junior employees are in charge of finding available temporary workers ("temps"). Junior employees are typically younger and communicate almost entirely by e-mail or by instant messaging. Senior managers often forget to open the instant messaging program, so they miss messages about which temps are available. The delays and missed messages are causing clients to go to competitors.

The Generation X office manager has proposed the following solutions:

01 The IT department can update the system settings so that the instant messaging program opens automatically when employees log in each morning.

02 The company can adopt "Face-to-Face Fridays" once a month. On these days, if employees are both in the office, they will have to speak with each other in person.

03 The company can create a "reverse" mentoring program that matches a younger employee with a senior employee to teach him or her how to use new technology to communicate in the workplace and to connect with clients.

TASK You are the CEO of Staffers Co. You want the employees to learn to be flexible in how they communicate and to choose the most efficient method based on the circumstances. Which of the three options do you instruct the office manager to put in place?

After reading this chapter, I can...
... start a conversation with unfamiliar people
... use basic conjunctions to convey deeper opinions
... brainstorm and discuss the pros and cons of different career choices

SNEAK PEAK: > How well do you keep track of time?

LESSON 01 / Breaking The Ice   15

LESSON 02
IT'S TIME!

OBJECTIVES

After this chapter, you will be able to...

- schedule time to meet someone
- use hour-first and minute-first time expressions to schedule meetings
- meet a co-worker after work

1 GETTING STARTED

A Let's look at the image.
Describe what's happening in the picture.

What is her body language telling us?

B Discuss the questions below:

> What time is it right now? What alternative ways can you say that?

> What expressions can you use to say you'll meet someone, but not at an exact minute or hour?

> What cultures have strict time commitments? Which have loose time commitments?

GOOD TO KNOW
Common Mistakes

Which is right? *Check your answers in the back of the book.*

> Do you have **a/ the** time?
> Thanks, I had **a/ the** great time!
> There's **a/ the** time for action, and **a/ the** time is now.

2 LANGUAGE PREVIEW

A Business Expressions
Read the following expressions and write your own sentence for each.

wrap up: complete a task.

E.g.) Let's wrap this up quickly; I have to be somewhere in an hour.

Make your own: _____

o'clock sharp: at exactly the hour.

E.g.) I start work at exactly eight o'clock sharp. Never later. Never earlier.

Make your own: _____

push something back: postpone.

E.g.) It looks like I can't make it on time. Do you mind pushing things back an hour?

Make your own: _____

B Key Patterns
Here are some key patterns that you can use when arranging time to meet someone.

I'm free…	I'm off by…	Let's say…
… anytime before 8 pm	… 6:00 pm	… 8:15
… after 6:30 pm	… 9 o'clock	… after work
… in the afternoon	… nightfall	… tomorrow at lunch

3 THE FORMAL SORT

A Formal or Informal?
With a partner, sort the expressions and explain why you believe it is formal or informal.

Do you have a moment?   Are you free?   At approximately five o'clock…
When would you like?   Around five-ish…   When's good?

Formal	Informal

LESSON 02 / It's Time! 17

4 INTERACTIONS

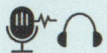 **A** Listen and fill in the blanks.

B Practice the dialogue with the options below.

Negotiating a Meeting Time

Anne: I'm free anytime this week after work.

Allen: When do you usually (1)_____?

Anne: Most days I'm off by (2)_____.

Allen: After 5:00 pm is fine. Okay, well, Tuesday (3)_____ for me.

Anne: I have a meeting at four o'clock that should (4)_____ by half-past five at the latest.

Allen: Let's say quarter to six?

Anne: 5:45 it is. (5)_____ meeting at the coffee shop on 8th Avenue?

Allen: That works for me.

Anne: I'll call you Tuesday morning to confirm.

Allen: Thanks, Anne.

Option 1
1. finish work
2. 5:00 o'clock
3. is good
4. finish
5. How about

Option 2
1. leave work
2. 5:00
3. is best
4. be over
5. What about

C Pragmatic Comprehension

01 What time expressions are used here?

02 What kind of relationship do you think these two people have?

03 How does Anne acknowledge plans might change?

"He finally had time to develop a marketing plan."

Grammar Brief ▸ p. 77

18 LESSON 02 / It's Time!

5 ATTENTIVE LISTENING

🎧 **Extended Dialogue** · *Two people are rescheduling an appointment.*

A **Listening Comprehension.** *Listen and complete the questions below.*

01 What idioms are used to talk about time?
_____
_____

02 How does the man feel about the woman rescheduling?
_____
_____

03 What time do they finally decide to meet?
_____
_____

B **Matching**
Match the utterances to the appropriate responses. With a partner to think of an alternative way of responding to the original utterance.

› Twenty to at the latest.	Would you rather meet up on tomorrow?
› I'm having dinner at 7:00 sharp.	So, 6:40 pm? Not a problem. *"That works."*
› I'll leave a 5:00 pm.	No worries.
› Sorry to cancel like this.	Thanks. I'm looking forward to meeting you.
› I need to move our meeting.	What time would you need to leave to get there?

(Twenty to at the latest. — So, 6:40 pm? Not a problem.)

Audio Script — p. 86

QUOTE OF THE DAY

"Time does not change us. It just unfolds us."
— Max Frisch

"They always say time changes things, but you actually have to change them yourself."
— Andy Warhol

> Has time changed or unfolded you? Why do you say so?

> What experience from your life can you give as an example of one of the above quotes?

LESSON 02 / It's Time!

6 BUSINESS BASICS

You and a friend want to meet up after work.
Look at the events posted on your city's entertainment website.

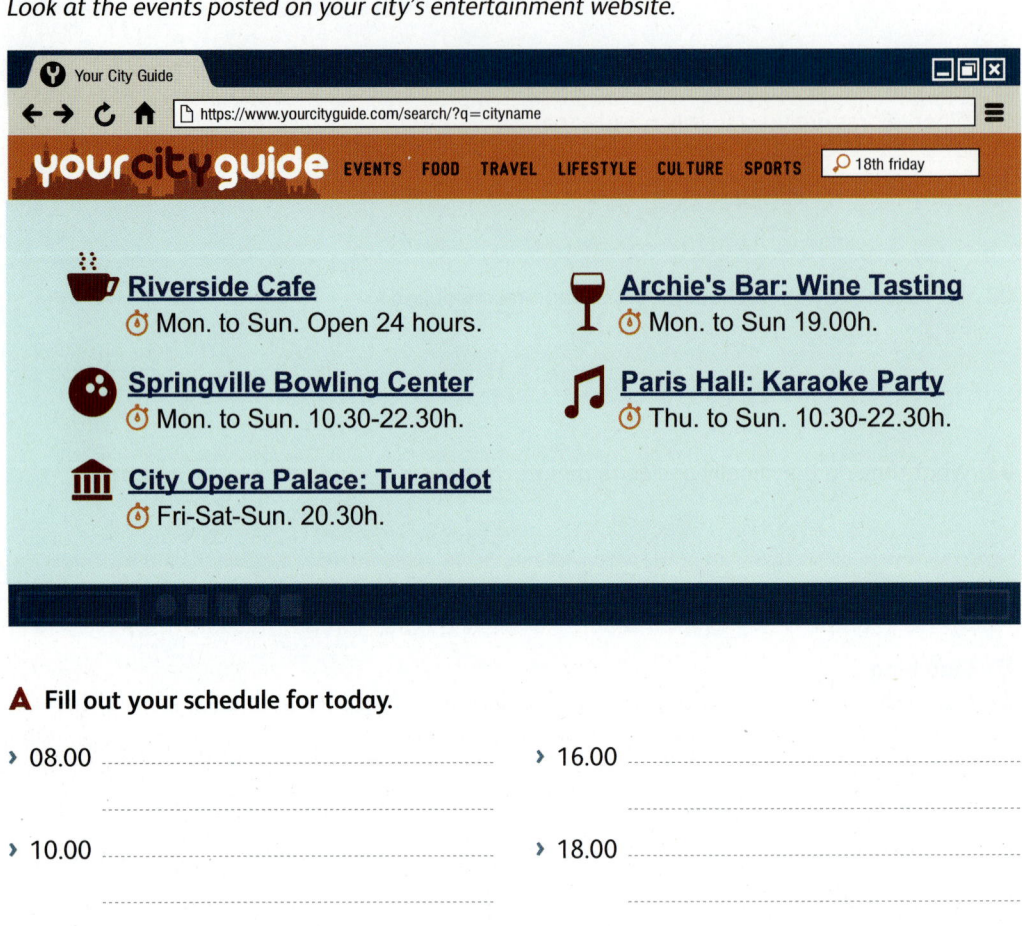

A Fill out your schedule for today.

> 08.00

> 10.00

> 12.00

> 14.00

> 16.00

> 18.00

> 20.00

> 22.00

B Work in pairs.
Look at the City Guide. Choose events that you and your partners would like to do and find potential times when you and your partners are free. Arrange your schedules as necessary.

Event	Time to arrive	Time to leave

7 TALKING SHOP

A Group Discussion
In groups, choose questions that interest you the most and discuss.

01 Are you a good manager of time or is time a good manager of you? Explain.
02 What is your daily routine like?
03 What time of day are you most/ least productive?
04 How do you deal with people who are regularly late?
05 What would you change in your daily schedule if you could?
06 Which time is most valuable to you: time with family, time at work, or time alone? Why? How would you rank them?
07 What do you think of people who are "fashionably late"?
08 Your own: _____

8 DILEMMA

You have been appointed as a leading efficiency specialist for Moobla, a medium-sized game developer. Your primary objective is to increase the productivity of a twenty-member team. Punctuality appears to be the leading area of concern. Team members come to meetings late or leave earlier to attend other meetings. Most recently, you scheduled a team meeting to start at 9:00 AM, but it took thirty minutes for all team members to gather. As the result, important points were missed and not all questions were discussed.

It seems that Moobla's informal culture does not value strict time frames. However, permitting unpredictable scheduling to continue may create angst between the members of your team and affect the overall efficiency of your work. This is your first significant issue to deal with and you would like to get started with your team on the right foot.

TASK Decide whether to act or allow this to continue. Explain what you will do and why you decided to do it.

After reading this chapter, I can...
... schedule time to meet someone
... use hour-first and minute-first time expressions to schedule meetings
... meet a co-worker after work

SNEAK PEAK: > How do you get to your favorite restaurant from here?

LESSON 02 / It's Time!

REVIEW 1

- [ ] Hold a conversation for three minutes. Start with an ice breaker.
- [ ] Use "can't imagine," "take a power nap," or "need a boost" in a sentence.
- [ ] Select a partner from your group. Choose a Key Pattern from Lesson 1 for your partner to use in a sentence.
- [ ] Evaluate your job. Provide at least one pro and one con in your evaluation.
- [ ] What time is it right now? Say it in at least two different ways.
- [ ] Make an appointment to meet a partner after class. Include the time and place.
- [ ] Use Key Patterns from Lesson 2 to make an appointment with your group.
- [ ] Choose a partner to say wrap up, o'clock sharp, or push something back in a sentence.
- [ ] Go back and answer questions you haven't done yet!

TIPS:
- Take turns answering questions with your team members.
- When you reach the end, go back and answer questions you skipped.

- [ ] **ALL DONE!**

LESSON 03 NAVIGATING YOUR AREA

OBJECTIVES

After this chapter, you will be able to...

- identify common places and features in an office building
- use prepositions to provide directions
- give directions to areas in an office

1 GETTING STARTED

A Let's look at the image.
Describe what's happening in the picture.

How can this man show he understands the directions being given

B Discuss the questions below:

› What places do you think people most often ask directions for in an office building?

› What rooms and features do you most commonly see in offices?

› What do you think the key is to providing good directions?

GOOD TO KNOW — Common Mistakes

Which is right? *Check your answers in the back of the book.*

› Of course I know how to get there. It's common **sense/ knowledge**!

› Not talking in an elevator is common **sense/ courtesy**.

› It's common **sense/ knowledge** that you shouldn't do business with a criminal.

2 LANGUAGE PREVIEW

A Business Expressions
Read the following expressions and write your own sentence for each.

wind down: in the final stages of a process, gadually preparing to finish.

E.g.) *I was a little late, so the meeting was winding down by the time I got there.*
Make your own: _____

catch someone next time: *informal.* meet someone at an unspecified later date.

E.g.) *Do you mind if I catch you guys next time? I've got a lot of work to do here.*
Make your own: _____

firm up: make plans more definite.

E.g.) *We're going to meet and firm up the agreement a bit. A few points are still unclear.*
Make your own: _____

B Key Patterns
Here are some key patterns that you can use when getting around.

Where might I find…?	It's… down…	It's right…
… the men's/ ladies room	… 2 doors… on your left	… next to the boardroom
… Matt from Billing	… all the way… the hall	… across the hall from reception
… the closest exit	… several blocks… this street	… past the copy machine

3 THE FORMAL SORT

A Formal or Informal?
With a partner, sort the expressions and explain why you believe it is formal or informal.

Could you tell me where…   Do you know where…   Sure, just go…
Certainly! Follow this hall…   Hang a left…   Turn left…

Formal	Informal

4 INTERACTIONS

 **A** Listen and fill in the blanks.

Asking at Reception

John: Excuse me, (1) _____ what room the staff meeting is in?

Rcpt.: Do you know where the (2) _____ is?

John: No, sorry, I'm new here.

Rcpt.: Ok, it's on the third floor. Take the elevator and (3) _____ as soon as you get off.

John: So it's right there?

Rcpt.: (4) _____, you'll have to walk past some workstations. It's the big office near the end of the hall.

John: I see. Which side is it on?

Rcpt.: The only place to go is right. Don't worry, you can't miss it.

John: Great; so third floor, (5) _____, end of the hall.

Rcpt.: That's right. Good luck!

B Practice the dialogue with the options below.

Option 1
1. could you tell me
2. boardroom
3. go left
4. Not quite
5. left

Option 2
1. do you know
2. copy room
3. make a right
4. No
5. right

C Pragmatic Comprehension

01 Is the receptionist behaving as you would expect? Why or why not?

02 How does John confirm the receptionist's instructions?

03 What are the different uses for "right" in this dialogue?

Grammar Brief p. 78

LESSON 03 / Navigating Your Area

5 ATTENTIVE LISTENING

🎧 **Extended Dialogue** · *An office worker has trouble getting to his meeting.*

A Active Listening. Think about the following questions as you listen. Write the answers in the spaces below.

› What trouble does John have?
....
....

› Why does John need to get to the meeting?
....
....

› What are John's directions?
....
....

B True or False. *Circle T for true and F for false. Explain your answer.*

01	John went to the wrong room.	T /(F)	*"False! The room was correct, but the meeting was changed."*
02	John wasn't sent an SMS message.	T / F	
03	The meeting is in the next building.	T / F	
04	The woman doesn't think John can make it to the meeting.	T / F	
05	The HR office is past John's destination.	T / F	

Audio Script ▸ p. 87

QUOTE OF THE DAY

› What do you think these quotations mean?

› How do these expressions apply to you?

"Life is a journey, not a destination."
— Unknown

"If you tell people where to go, but not how to get there, you'll be amazed at the results."
— George S. Patton

LESSON 03 / Navigating Your Area

6 BUSINESS BASICS

A Labeling
Draw lines linking features in the diagram with the appropriate terms on the right.

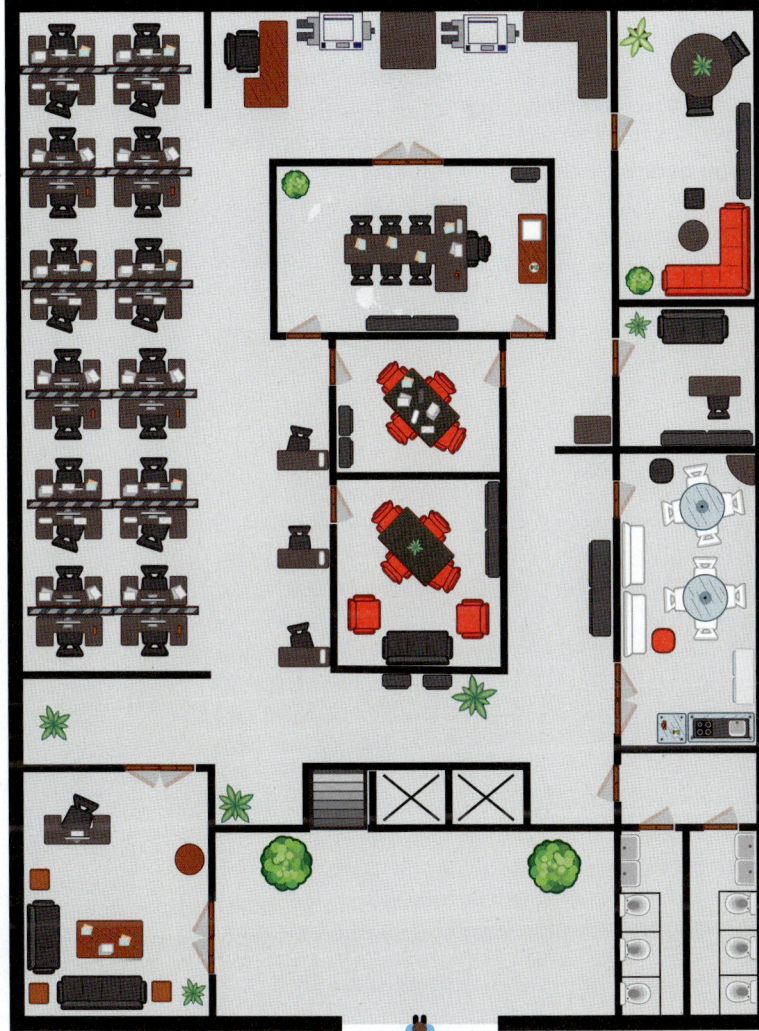

› office lounge
› copy machine(s)
› work station(s)
› meeting room(s)
› boardroom
› ergonomic chair(s)
› greenery
› breakroom
› restrooms
› lobby
› office
› entrance/exit
› foyer

JOHN

B Giving Directions
John, the new office assistant, has errands to run before people get to the office. Look at John's to-do list and take turns with a partner telling him where to go.

To Do:
- *make copies of morning report*
- *put copies in boardroom*
- *water the greenery*
- *make coffee in breakroom*
- *your own:*

LESSON 03 / Navigating Your Area

7 TALKING SHOP

A Group Discussion
In groups, choose questions that interest you the most and discuss.

01 Sometimes people don't know the directions to where you would like to go, but still tell you how to get there. What experience do you have with this?

02 If you have time, is it better to ask for directions or find a place on your own? Why?

03 What do you do when you clearly see that someone is lost?

04 How can you tell if a person knows or doesn't know the directions they give you?

05 What do you think of the idea that bad directions lead to good detours?

06 Do men and women process directions differently? How do you know?

07 What were the worst directions you ever received or gave? What happened as a result?

08 Your own: _____

8 CASE STUDY

Meppy, a map application for portable devices, has recently experienced a threat to its public image and financial operations. A user in St. Louis, Lorna Weston, was using the application to help her find a walking path to a nearby hotel when she was provided the wrong location. Meppy's directions said Ms. Weston was behind a location when she was actually several blocks in front of it. The map then zoomed several more blocks away and indicated that she needed to turn down a street into an underdeveloped neighborhood. Soon after entering the neighborhood, Ms. Weston was robbed. She sustained minor physical injuries and lost her wallet with all of its contents.

Meppy is aware of the application's tracking glitches and the company has been trying to fix it. Even prior to this incident, Meppy included a disclaimer on its directions stating that the software is in beta mode and that tracking may not always be accurate. The company fears that negative publicity from this incident and a potential lawsuit will harm its public perception and damage its position in the highly competitive navigation market.

Three options are being discussed at company headquarters:

01 Take the application down. Pay Ms. Weston "an undisclosed sum" for her troubles.

02 Keep the application running. Pay Ms. Weston "an undisclosed sum" for her troubles.

03 Keep the application running. Let your legal team handle it and follow the court's decision.

TASK With your team, discuss the effects of each potential choice and identify the best course of action to follow.

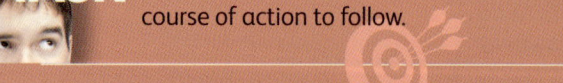

After reading this chapter, I can...
... identify common places and features in an office building
... use prepositions to provide directions
... give directions to areas in an office

SNEAK PEAK: > What's trending right now?

04 TRENDING TOPICS

OBJECTIVES

After this chapter, you will be able to...

- communicate basic trends on a graph
- use simple past, present perfect, and dummy subjects for market analysis
- explain a line graph

1 GETTING STARTED

A Let's look at the image.
Describe what's happening in the picture.

What in your life could this upward trend represent?

B Discuss the questions below:

› What is difficult about explaining graphs in English?

› What topics are trending lately?

› What trends were popular last year that aren't trending this year?

GOOD TO KNOW
Common Mistakes

Which is right? *Check your answers in the back of the book.*

› How / **What** do you think about the market?
› How / **What** do you know about that?
› **How** / What can you solve this problem?

2 LANGUAGE PREVIEW

A Business Expressions
Read the following expressions and write your own sentence for each.

level off: stay the same after a previous period of gains or decline.

E.g.) The market has finally leveled off after a week of steady gains.
Make your own: ....

bottom out: hit the lowest point.

E.g.) After a long decline, the stocks finally bottomed out at $2 per share.
Make your own: ....

take a hit: suddenly get worse, especially as a result of something.

E.g.) After airing a series of boring shows, the network's ratings took a hit.
Make your own: ....

B Key Patterns
Here are some key patterns that you can use to explain trends on a line graph.

... hit a peak of...	This... tells us...	As you can see...
Sales... around $12,000 The stock... just over $17 Funding... $3m	... pie chart... each party's contribution ... line graph... an increase in spending ... bar graph... total visitors each year	... sales rose 30% ... stock prices declined ... more people chose bottled water

3 THE FORMAL SORT

A Formal or Informal?
With a partner, sort the expressions and explain why you believe it is formal or informal.

There has been an increase in sales.   Sales are going up.   Stocks went down quickly.
Stocks fell sharply.   Rates remained steady.   Rates stayed the same.

Formal	Informal
....	....
....	....
....	....

4 INTERACTIONS

 **A** Listen and fill in the blanks.

Market Trends

Grant: As you can see by the blue line, annual sales (1)_____ in 2010.

Grace: Sorry, I can't (2)_____. What did they bottom out at?

Grant: $(3)_____. But then there was a gradual rise in sales that peaked at $400,000.

Grace: Since then they've more or less (4)_____.

Grant: Exactly, but not for our (5)_____.

Grace: Is the red line R. Motors?

Grant: That's B. Automotives. R. Motors is the green line.

Grace: It looks like they're (6)_____ in different directions.

Grant: But we're staying the same.

Grace: Okay, so let's discuss how to keep up with B. Automotives.

B Practice the dialogue with the options below.

Option 1
1. hit their lowest point
2. see that
3. 14,000
4. flattened out
5. competition
6. moving

Option 2
1. plummeted
2. make that out
3. 40,000
4. plateaued
5. rivals
6. headed

C Pragmatic Comprehension

01 What kind of meeting is this?

02 What kind of market do Grant and Grace work in?

03 How are each of the companies trending?

Grammar Brief ▶ p. 79

"Looks like you are feeling better."

LESSON 04 / Trending Topics 31

5 ATTENTIVE LISTENING

🎧 **Extended Dialogue** · *An office worker asks a colleague how a stock has performed over the last year.*

A Listen to the dialogue and draw the stock's trend on the graph below.

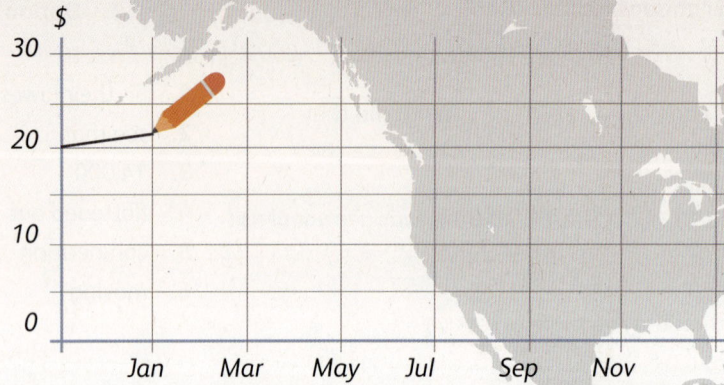

B With a partner, answer the questions below.

01 What is the stock currently valued at?

02 Have there been many changes in the stock's value? What were they?

03 When was the stock stable?

04 Does Grant think Janet should invest in the stock?

 Would you buy this stock? Why?

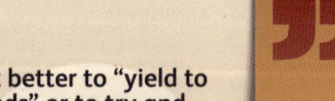

QUOTE OF THE DAY

"Great things are not accomplished by those who yield to trends and fads and popular opinion."

— Jack Kerouac

"Follow sound business trends, not fashion trends."

— Janice Dickinson

> Is it better to "yield to trends" or to try and make your own? Why?
> What does it take to create a trend? What trends have you helped create?

6 BUSINESS BASICS

A Complete the Chart
Read "Companies in Contrast" and draw the company stock trends on the line chart provided.

COMPANIES IN CONTRAST
A TALE OF THREE COMPANIES

Dongler started the year at $45 per share and gradually increased to it's current price of $55 per share. It had a brief spike in October, peaking around $60 and dipped briefly in November.

Binker was more volatile. It began the year at $40, but took a hit after firing its CEO in February. The stock plummeted and bottomed out at $15. It fluctuated over the next two months, but gradually started to improve in late April. The stock has almost recovered and now sits at $35 per share.

B Complete the Article
Look at Oodle's trends in the graph above and describe in the lines.

Oodles started the year around…

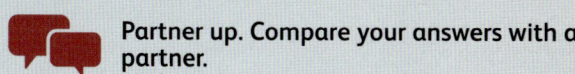

Partner up. Compare your answers with a partner.

LESSON 04 / Trending Topics   33

7 TALKING SHOP

A Group Discussion
In groups, choose questions that interest you the most and discuss.

01 What companies would you consider trend setters? What makes them different?

02 What is the biggest trend of the last five years that you didn't follow? Why did you avoid it?

03 Which trend has had the most influence in your life?

04 What trend are you most embarrassed being a part of?

05 Think of a company that has steadily trended upward for decades. What made it so successful?

06 How do you think successful investors do so well in the stock market?

07 What is the most popular tech company at the moment? How long do you think they will stay at the top? Why?

08 Your own: _____

8 CASE STUDY

Since 2006, German automaker, Nobel, has enjoyed a steady rise in the global demand for its vehicles. This demand is in part due to its stylish, modern designs, but also due to its manufacturing. Nobel prides itself on making reliable vehicles and only manufactures vehicles in German locations where it can ensure quality control. Its brand has increasingly become associated with reliability and precision.

Despite an overall increase in global demand, the European market has recently bottomed out after six years of decline. Consequently, it is crucial that the German automaker focus on the global market for its vehicles in order to make up for the decline in local demand. However, in order to meet global demand, particularly the markets in the US and China, Nobel must expand its production. This means producing a percentage of vehicles offshore.

In addition to concerns about quality, Nobel fears how local perception and negative publicity may affect the company's image. It also fears that if the company does not outsource, that it will lose market share that it has worked hard to get.

TASK You are part of the CEO's advisory committee. Discuss what direction the company should take and why. Should they expand production outside of Germany or maintain control over quality and public perception by keeping manufacturing local?

After reading this chapter, I can...
... communicate basic trends on a graph
... use simple past, present perfect, and dummy subjects for market analysis
... explain a line graph

SNEAK PEAK: > What's the difference between want, hope, and dream?

REVIEW 2

- [ ] Ask directions to room or area in your building.
- [ ] Give directions to your favorite restaurant, cafeteria, or quiet area around you.
- [ ] Choose someone from your group to use "wind down," "firm up," or "catch someone next time" in a sentence.
- [ ] Describe an upward or downward trend in your industry. Why is it trending that way?
- [ ] Have a conversation with your group. Use the three Key Patterns from Lesson 3 in your discussion.
- [ ] Talk about a market trend that has recently fluctuated or leveled off. What would improve its performance?
- [ ] Use "level off," "bottom out," or "take a hit" in a conversation with a partner.
- [ ] Ask a group member to say "hit a peak of," "this tells us," or "as you can see" in a sentence.
- [ ] Go back and answer any questions you haven't answered yet!

TIPS:
- Take turns answering questions with your team members.
- When you reach the end, go back and answer questions you haven't answered.

- [ ] **ALL DONE!**

LESSON 05
EVERYTHING YOU WANT

OBJECTIVES

After this chapter, you will be able to…

- talk about wants, hopes, and dreams
- use present perfect continuous to communicate desires and goals
- explain your goals on a timeline

1 GETTING STARTED

A Let's look at the image.
Describe what's happening in the picture.

Which word best describes what this man's desire: hope, want, wish, dream?

B Discuss the questions below:

> What other body language shows desire?

> What gestures do you make when you tell people what you want?

> What role do gestures play in communicating your desires?

GOOD TO KNOW
Common Mistakes

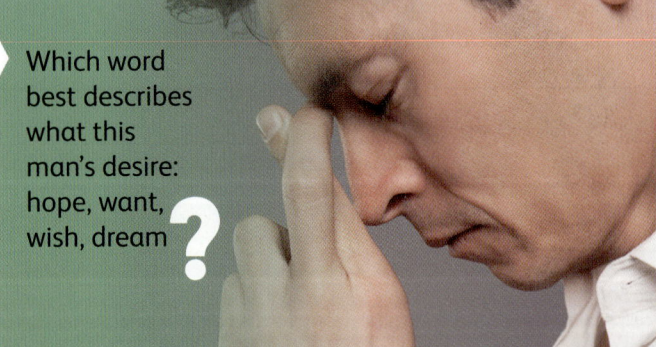

Which is right? *Circle the correct answer in bold. Check the answers in the back of the book.*

> Hi Bob, I'll see you **in ten minutes / ten minutes later**.

> Jane and Michael will get married next year. **In nine months / nine months later** they'll have a baby.

> The meeting will finish **in twenty minutes / twenty minutes later** today.

2 LANGUAGE PREVIEW

A Business Expressions
Read the following expressions and write your own sentence for each.

could use something : desire something, especially to relieve stress.

E.g.) Work has been too hectic the last few months. I could really use a vacation.

Make your own: _____

have an ulterior motive: have a hidden reason for doing something.

E.g.) Politicians may have ulterior motives for doing things, especially during election season.

Make your own: _____

count someone in: to include someone.

E.g.) If you're putting together a special task force, count me in. I'd love to be part of it.

Make your own: _____

B Key Patterns
Here are some key patterns that you can use when expressing your desires.

My dream is to...	I've been wanting to...	Keep... and I'll keep...
... open up a restaurant	... ask you	... your US dollars... my gold
... retire while I'm young	... get promoted for a bit	... producing... paying
... have a large family	... get that report finished	... your beliefs... mine

3 THE FORMAL SORT

A Formal or Informal?
With a partner, sort the expressions and explain why you believe it is formal or informal.

I hope to...
It would have been be of benefit to...
My dream is to...
I aspire to...
I wish I could have...
My greatest desire is to...

Formal

_____

_____

_____

Informal

_____

_____

_____

LESSON 05 / Everything You Want

4 INTERACTIONS

 **A** Listen and fill in the blanks.

Visiting a friendly Co-worker

Ruth: Hey (1) _____, what's going on in here?

Mark: Hey! Nothing out of the ordinary. Just (2) _____.

Ruth: I could really use a (3) _____. I've been wanting to get out of here since lunch.

Mark: And I've been wanting to sleep since I got up, (4) _____ here we are.

Ruth: You know, there's a way to solve this problem.

Mark: Retirement?

Ruth: Now you're talking. Most people in here have been secretly hoping for that merger with Genetix... and a nice severance package.

Mark: Keep dreaming and I'll keep working.

Ruth: All right, I'll let you get back. But let me know if you change your mind.

Mark: Will do. Thanks for (5) _____.

B Practice the dialogue with the options below.

Option 1

1. Mark
2. working hard
3. cigarette
4. yet
5. dropping by

Option 2

1. buddy
2. getting some work done
3. break
4. still
5. saying hello

C Pragmatic Comprehension

01 Why does Mark stop by Ruth's office?

02 How do the two people communicate their desires?

03 What was the benefit to this conversation?

Grammar Brief ▶ p. 80

5 ATTENTIVE LISTENING

🎧 **Extended Dialogue** · *Three co-workers talk near an exit at work as they wait for the weather to improve.*

A Active Listening. Think about the following questions as you listen. Write the answers in the spaces below.

› Why did Ruth invite Mark to the bar? ....

› What does Mark think of Ruth's plans? ....

› Does Ruth want to change careers? ....

B True or False. *Circle T for true and F for false. Explain your answer.*

01	Ruth first suggests a familiar bar.	T (F)	"False! Ruth has been wanting to go to a new place called Momo's."
02	Mark is feeling stressed.	T / F	
03	Ruth is interested in working at Momo's.	T / F	
04	Ruth wants to quit her job.	T / F	
05	Ruth values Mark's opinion.	T / F	

 What do you think will happen next?

Audio Script ▸ p. 88

QUOTE OF THE DAY

› How are these quotations related (or not related)?

› Which quote best represents your belief? Why?

"Everything that is done in the world is done by hope."

— Martin Luther

"Hope in reality is the worst of all evils because it prolongs the torments of man."

— Friedrich Nietzsche

LESSON 05 / Everything You Want   39

6 BUSINESS BASICS

A **Timeline of Desires**
Choose four points on the timeline and write one desire for each. Include one past desire that did not come true..

I wish...	I want....

I hope...	I dream...

earlier — now — next year — 5 years from now — retirement

B **Pair work.**
Take turns with a partner discussing your timelines. Take notes about your partner to share with the class.

7 TALKING SHOP

A Group Discussion
In groups, choose questions that interest you the most and discuss.

01 What is your greatest hope for you, your family, or your friends?
02 What is your dream? Do you think you'll be able to achieve it? Why?
03 What is your ultimate career goal?
04 What dreams of yours have come true so far?
05 What position do you want in the next 5 years? What will it take to achieve that?
06 Do you still chase dreams that haven't come true? If yes, will you ever give up? If no, what made you stop?
07 If you could make one career wish come true for someone you know, what would it be?
08 Your own: ....

8 CASE STUDY

You have recently been promoted to the brand manager position at work. Breaking into management has long been a dream of yours and you have been working toward it since entering the company five years ago. However, even though you were happy to receive the promotion, it has been making things awkward between you and your former peers. While you worked well together before and still consider them close friends, they have not been taking you seriously as a manger. They often start late or socialize for extended periods. Additionally, they tend to complain about pay and scheduling. You have been trying to remain patient, yet things need to change.

Your most trusted colleagues suggest the following:

01 Schedule a staff meeting to discuss the transition. Ask the team for their input on how to make the transition to new roles a positive and effective one.

02 Meet with your team individually. Provide clear expectations you have for them as a manager.

03 Request a transfer. Deal with the situation until you can transfer out.

TASK Discuss which option would be the most suitable for you.

After reading this chapter, I can...
... talk about wants, hopes, and dreams
... use present perfect continuous to communicate desires and goals
... explain your goals on a timeline

SNEAK PEAK: > What is the most recent problem you have had with technology in the workplace?

LESSON 05 / *Everything You Want*

LESSON

06
WHAT HAPPENED?

 OBJECTIVES

After this chapter, you will be able to...

- explain a past action that was interrupted
- use the simple past tense with the past continuous tense to explain two simultaneous actions
- complete and explain a product problem form

1 GETTING STARTED

A Let's look at the image.
Describe what's happening in the picture.

What are these two people thinking?

B Discuss the questions below:

› What are common computer related troubles people often have?

› When do you feel angriest at your computer?

› Will there ever be a time when people no longer have trouble with technology? Why?

GOOD TO KNOW
Common Mistakes

Which is right? *Circle the correct words in bold. Check the answers in the back of the book.*

› A: When will you go?
  B: **I don't know about that/ I don't know.**

› A: It won't rain at all next month.
  B: **I don't know about that/ I don't know.**

› A: Coffee was thrown out of your window.
  B: Well, **I don't know about that/ I don't know.**

2 LANGUAGE PREVIEW

A Business Expressions
Read the following expressions and write your own sentence for each.

get your hopes up: be overly optimistic about an outcome.

E.g.) I wouldn't get your hopes up over a raise. Financially, the company has had a horrible year.

Make your own: _____

have a look: examine something to find the problem.

E.g.) Your computer crashed again? Let me have a look; I might be able to fix it.

Make your own: _____

nip something in the bud: stop a potential problem from becoming an actual problem.

E.g.) Misbehavior should be nipped in the bud before it spreads throughout your entire team.

Make your own: _____

B Key Patterns
Here are some key patterns that you can use when explaining problems and getting something fixed.

I was... when...	I tried... but...	Could you... when you're done?
... typing an e-mail... my PC crashed	... restarting... it didn't help	... call me
... driving to work... a car hit me	... contacting him... didn't hear back	... e-mail me
... saving a file... my computer shut down	... calling... couldn't reach him	... text me

3 THE FORMAL SORT

A Formal or Informal?
With a partner, sort the expressions and explain why you believe it is formal or informal.

The problem was...   I tried to...   The inconvenience was...
Of course...   I attempted to...   Most assuredly...

Formal	Informal

LESSON 06 / What Happened?

4 INTERACTIONS

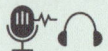 **A** Listen and fill in the blanks.

What Happened?

Quinn: What happened?

Paige: I was updating my software when the screen froze.

Quinn: Did you try restarting it?

Paige: Yeah, restarting didn't help. I tried turning the power off and on. No luck.

Quinn: You're the second person today with that (1) _____. I'll have a look.

Paige: Do you think you (2) _____ fix it by the end of the day?

Quinn: I'll try, but I wouldn't get my hopes up. That's actually what I was working on when you (3) _____ in.

Paige: Ugh. When it crashed, I was working on a (4) _____. It has all my files.

Quinn: You didn't save to the cloud?

Paige: That's what the update was for!

Quinn: (5) _____ ... sorry. I'll do my best.

Paige: That's all I can ask. Here's my card; could you call me at this number when (6) _____?

B Practice the dialogue with the options below.

Option 1

1. issue
2. could
3. stopped
4. report
5. That's unfortunate
6. it's ready

Option 2

1. trouble
2. might be able to
3. dropped
4. document
5. Ouch
6. it's ready to go

C Pragmatic Comprehension

01 How serious is the issue?

02 Should Paige expect her computer to be fixed the same day? How do you know?

03 Why was Quinn sorry?

Grammar Brief p. 81

"While I was planting some bulbs today, I dug up an ancient civilization."

44 LESSON 06 / What Happened?

5 ATTENTIVE LISTENING

🎧 **Extended Dialogue** · *Two co-workers discuss computer troubles at work.*

A **Listening Comprehension.** *Listen and complete the questions below.*

› What is the problem?

› Who was Quinn e-mailing?

› What will Quinn and Vicky do next?

B **Matching**
Match the utterances to the appropriate responses. With a partner to think of an alternative way of responding to the original utterance.

› I found a bug in the software.   No kidding.
› Let's nip this in the bud.   That's bad news. *"That's unfortunate."*
› Four others had the same issue.   I'll just send somebody else.
› Hopefully I can make it tomor-   Hopefully we won't have anymore problems.
   row.
› Can you still go?   I'll let people know.

Audio Script ▸ p. 88

QUOTE OF THE DAY

"Man only likes to count his troubles; he doesn't calculate his happiness."

Fyodor Dostoyevsky

"My mother had a great deal of trouble with me, but I think she enjoyed it."

Mark Twain

› What good can come out of difficult times?

› Which quote do you better identify with? Why?

LESSON 06 / What Happened?

6 BUSINESS BASICS

A Product Problem Return Form.
What was the last defective item you purchased (personal or work-related)?
Fill out the form with its information.

To Return; Please fill in Item Number, quantity returned and reason code as described below.

Reason Codes
1 - Incorrect Item   2 - Item Damaged   3 - Item Arrived Late
4 - Other (Please Explain)

Ordered by:
First Name:
Last Name:
Address:
City:
State: Zip Code:

Order Details
Order Date:
Ship Date:
Sales Order No.:
Page No.:

Item	Description	Reason Code	Remarks

B With a partner.
Ask your partner about the problem using the questions below.

01 What was the problem?

02 What happened?

03 Did you try to solve the problem? If yes, how?

LESSON 06 / What Happened?

7 TALKING SHOP

A Group Discussion
In groups, choose questions that interest you the most and discuss.

01 Who do you usually go to when you have trouble at work? Why?

02 What are the most common work-related problems you have?

03 Do people usually turn to you for help? Why?

04 What advice do you give someone when their problem is unsolvable?

05 What is the biggest trouble at work that you've had to overcome? What happened?

06 What do you do when someone needs your help but you are busy?

07 What is the best way to deal with stress at work?

08 Your own: ....

8 DILEMMA

Mario Rossi and Aldo Bianchi are graphic designers at the Madrid-based marketing company, Miro. They were sent on a business trip to Paris to assist Miro's marketing director in a presentation for a new, blue chip client. The designers left the Madrid office together, but arrived separately. Something has gone wrong and they are presently not talking to one another.

Talking separately with both, Rossi explains that on the way to Paris he saw Bianchi copying files from Rossi's computer. Rossi is convinced that Bianchi was stealing his designs and wanted to use these designs for his own advancement. Bianchi claims that he was using Rossi's computer because he had to finish a logo and his own computer was not functioning properly. Due to the accusations, the designers refuse to work together any longer. The time for the presentation is rapidly approaching and it is crucial that this conflict does not affect its outcome.

The marketing director calls the head office to inform you of the situation and ask for advice. He explains Rossi is the leading designer on the project and is to present the overall concept to the client. Bianchi worked on specific details of the design and is more capable of answering specific questions of the clients. Both are critical to present a professional, reliable image to the client.

TASK Review the situation with your team and offer a solution to the marketing director.

After reading this chapter, I can...
... explain a past action that was interrupted
... use the simple past tense with the past continuous tense to explain two simultaneous actions
... complete and explain a product problem form

SNEAK PEAK: > What do people usually ask you for help on?

LESSON 06 / What Happened?

REVIEW 3

- ☐ Use examples from your life to explain the difference between hope, want, and dream.

- ☐ For two minutes, talk about something you have been wanting to do for a long time.

- ☐ Ask a partner to use "My dream is to," "I've been wanting to," or "keep... and I'll keep" in a sentence.

- ☐ Talk about a time you had an ulterior motive, discuss something you "could really use," or use "count someone in" in a sentence.

- ☐ Talk about a time that you were doing something that was interrupted. What happened?

- ☐ Discuss a recent problem you experienced and what you did to solve it.

- ☐ Use a Key Pattern from Chapter 6 in a conversation with your group.

- ☐ Go back and answer any questions you haven't answered yet!

- ☐ Start a conversation with your group. Use "get your hopes up," have a look, or "nip in the bud" in the discussion.

☐ **ALL DONE!**

TIPS:
- Take turns answering questions with your team members.
- When you reach the end, go back and answer questions you haven't answered.

LESSON 07
GETTING SOME HELP

OBJECTIVES

After this chapter, you will be able to...

- ask for help
- use politeness strategies to make requests
- politely ask for help or deny help if unable to provide it

1 GETTING STARTED

A Let's look at the image.
Describe what's happening in the picture.

How can you improve office collaboration?

B Discuss the questions below:

› How would you deal with someone who asks for help too often?

› When was the last time you asked for help? What was it for?

› Are some cultures more helpful than others?

GOOD TO KNOW
Common Mistakes

Which is right? Circle the correct answer. Check the answers in the back of the book.

› Need help? **What's wrong/ what's wrong with you**?

› Why are you being so rude? **What's wrong/ What's wrong with you**?

› You look upset. **What's wrong/ what's wrong with you**?

2 LANGUAGE PREVIEW

A Business Expressions
Read the following expressions and write your own sentence for each.

give someone a hand: help someone.

E.g.) Do you mind giving me a hand? I need help finishing this report.

Make your own: ....

look right: have the correct appearance; be accurate.

E.g.) I don't know if it's the grammar or the vocabulary, but something just doesn't look right.

Make your own: ....

come up with: invent, think of.

E.g.) After a productive brainstorming session, the team came up with some great ideas.

Make your own: ....

B Key Patterns
Here are some key patterns that you can use when asking for and giving help.

Would you mind…?	I need you to…	You might want to…
… giving me a hand	… send an e-mail	… use a spell checker
… helping me	… get back to me soon	… try another way
… writing an e-mail	… help me with something	… call someone else

3 THE FORMAL SORT

A Formal or Informal?
With a partner, sort the expressions and explain why you believe it is formal or informal.

Would you mind…   Can you…   Unfortunately, there's no way I could…
Sure, what's up?   No, not at all.   Sorry, I'm a little busy.

Formal	Informal

LESSON 07 / Getting Some Help

4 INTERACTIONS

 **A** Listen and fill in the blanks.

Getting Help with an E-mail

Will: Would you mind (1) _____ me with something?

Liz: Sure, what's up?

Will: I need you to (2) _____ an e-mail for me. Does this look right to you?

Liz: Yeah, but you might want to change the valediction.

Will: (3) _____ ?

Liz: Valediction. The (4) _____ words in your e-mail.

Will: Why? What's wrong with my "valediction?"

Liz: "(5) _____" sounds bossy.

Will: I couldn't come up with anything else. What can I say instead?

Liz: Try, "(6) _____." It's a lot friendlier.

B Practice the dialogue with the options below.

Option 1
1. giving me a hand
2. take a look at
3. Pardon
4. end
5. Hurry up
6. Please be expeditious

Option 2
1. helping me out
2. check
3. What do you mean
4. final
5. respond soon
6. at your earliest convenience

C Pragmatic Comprehension

01 Do these employees know each other? Why do you think so?

02 How does Liz feel about helping Will?

03 How does Will feel about Liz's advice?

Grammar Brief ▸ p. 82

LESSON 07 / Getting Some Help

5 ATTENTIVE LISTENING

🎧 **Extended Dialogue** · *A co-worker asks for more help with his writing.*

A **Active Listening.** Think about the following questions as you listen. Write the answers in the spaces below.

› Why does Liz say, "anytime" to Will? ....

› How do you know if Liz wants to help Will? ....

› What isn't Will undersanding? ....

B **True or False.** *Circle T for true and F for false. Explain your answer.*

01	Liz will help Will anytime.	T /(F)	"False! She was just being friendly."
02	Will hates asking Liz for help.	T / F	
03	Will doesn't like Ben.	T / F	
04	Will prefers to get help from people he knows.	T / F	
05	Liz is going to help Will one last time.	T / F	

❓ What do you think will happen next?

Audio Script ▸ p. 89

QUOTE OF THE DAY

› Do you agree with these quotes? Why or why not?

› Are the East and West different in their idea of helping others? Why do you think so?

"The purpose of life is not to be happy. It is to be useful, to be honorable, to be compassionate, to have it make some difference that you have lived and lived well."

Ralph Waldo Emerson

"Our prime purpose in this life is to help others. And if you can't help them, at least don't hurt them."

Dalai Lama

6 BUSINESS BASICS

A Write a list of things you currently need help with.

1. _____
2. _____
3. _____
4. _____

B Ask your partner for help based on the points from Section A.
Respond appropriately with the guide below.

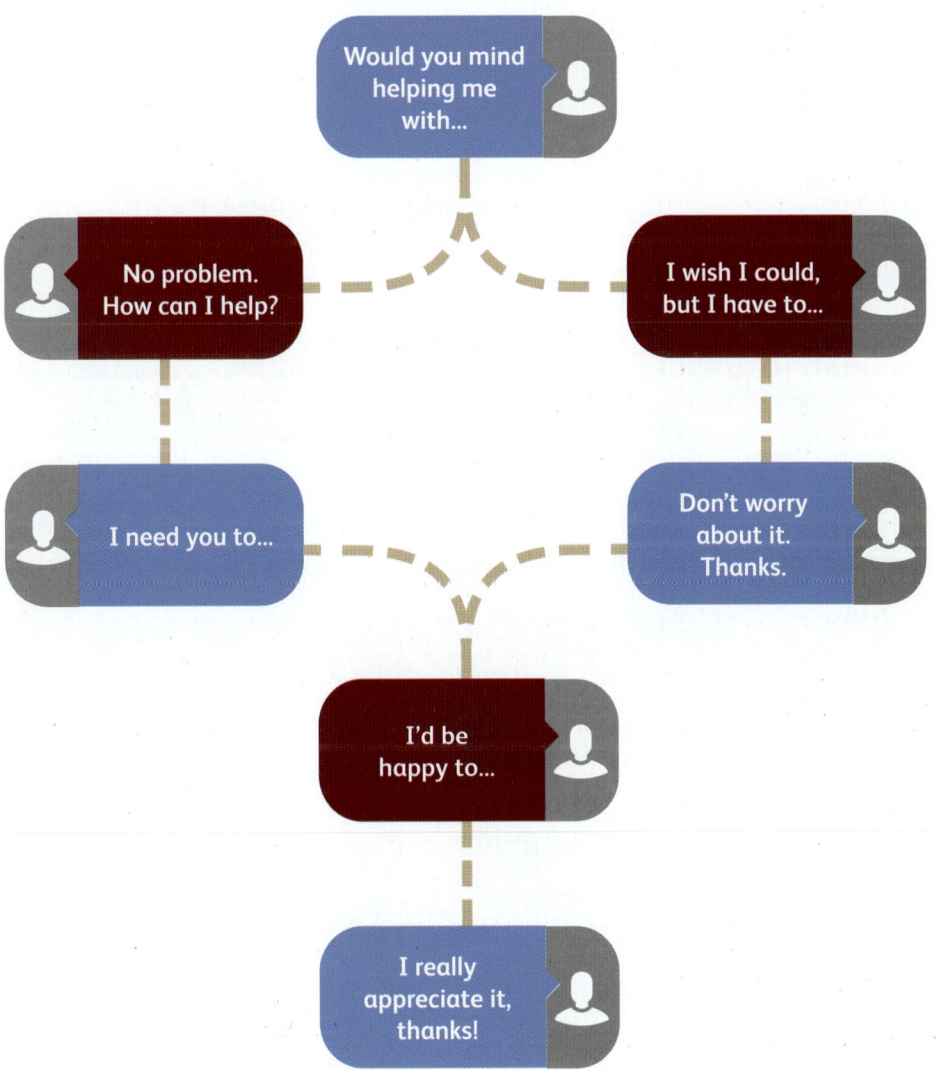

7 TALKING SHOP

A Group Discussion
In groups, choose questions that interest you the most and discuss.

01 Many companies have programs to help their communities. How does this help companies? Give an example from your experience.

02 Is it wise to help people you don't know? Why?

03 Do you feel comfortable asking for help? Why?

04 What volunteer work have you done? How has it helped you?

05 People who help others are called philanthropists. Who is the most famous philanthropist you know of? What have they done?

06 Do you ever give money to charity? Why or why not?

07 Is society becoming more or less responsible for others? Why do you think so?

08 Your own: _____

8 CASE STUDY

Pykup, a startup founded in 2012, is part of a tech-driven community in San Francisco. Pykup became popular through its peer-to-peer cell phone application that connects people who want car rides with people who can provide them. Since its creation, Pykup has carefully developed an image of being friendly and accessible to the community. Currently, there is a growing hostility toward the San Francisco tech industry. Locals feel that it is driving up housing prices and making the cost of living unmanageable. Pykup Public Relations sees this as an opportunity to promote its corporate culture and sidestep anger directed at local tech giants.

The Director of Public Relations suggests the following initiatives:

01 Donate a percentage of revenues to local charities, with emphasis on low-income housing.

02 Run a nationwide campaign providing rides and delivery services to people in need and charitable organizations.

03 Create a national advertising campaign that highlights regular contributions its drivers make to their communities.

TASK You are a member of the executive committee. Which option do you support? Discuss the pros and cons with your fellow committee members to come up with a solution.

After reading this chapter, **I can...**
... ask for help
... use politeness strategies to make requests
... politely ask for help or deny help if unable to provide it

SNEAK PEAK: > What differences in etiquette can you think of between your culture and American culture?

LESSON
08
PROPER CONDUCT

OBJECTIVES

After this chapter, you will be able to...

- identify common Western etiquette practices
- use type 2 conditionals to give advice
- recognize and discuss acceptable manners while dining

1 GETTING STARTED

A Let's look at the image.
Describe what's happening in the picture.

What is a more accepted way of eating this?

B Discuss the questions below:

› Why is it important to understand the etiquette of other cultures?

› What business etiquette tips can you think of? Take a minute to brainstorm.

› What happens when someone doesn't follow the tips you gave in the previous question?

GOOD TO KNOW
Common Mistakes

What's does it really mean? *The points below have specific (and odd) meanings. What are they? Check the answers in the back of the book.*

› I like dog.
› Let's go restaurant.
› Everyone ate some. It was a communism dish.

2 LANGUAGE PREVIEW

A Business Expressions
Read the following expressions and write your own sentence for each.

follow someone's lead: do as someone else does.

E.g.) I follow my boss's lead for working time; I wait until he leaves before I go home.

Make your own: _____

dig something up: find something after extensive searching.

E.g.) Even after googling the client, I wasn't able to dig up much information.

Make your own: _____

look into: research facts about something.

E.g.) Once Ted developed his business plan, he looked into getting a license.

Make your own: _____

B Key Patterns
Here are some key patterns that you can use when discussing advice.

If someone... do the same.	I'll be sure to...	I've got to say...
... orders a drink...	... try that	... that works for me
... texts back immediately...	... heed your advice	... that's quite insightful
... compliments you...	... give that a shot	... I can't see myself doing that

3 THE FORMAL SORT

A Formal or Informal?
With a partner, sort the expressions and explain why you believe it is formal or informal.

To me, it's absolutely unacceptable to...   You can't...   I have no issue with it.

It's all right.   As opposed to..., you should...   Instead of..., just...

Formal	Informal

LESSON 08 / Proper Conduct

4 INTERACTIONS

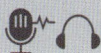 **A** Listen and fill in the blanks.

Dinner with the CEO

Troy: I've got to say, dinner with the CEO is a little (1) _____ . I don't even know what fork to use.

Claire: You don't have to. Just start from the outside and work your way in.

Troy: All right, I can do that. Let's keep the advice rolling.

Claire: Okay, avoid (2) _____ your phone, texting, or anything like that. In fact, just turn it off.

Troy: I'll be sure to do that. What about alcohol? It might calm the nerves a bit.

Claire: If I were you I'd follow Mr. Thompson's lead. If he orders a drink, (3) _____ .

Troy: That's great, but what do I even (4) _____ with him?

Claire: The website has a lot of (5) _____ on him. You could probably dig something up there.

Troy: I'll _____ that, thanks.

Claire: And last but not least, you absolutely cannot eat with your mouth open!

B Practice the dialogue with the options below.

Option 1

1. intimidating
2. getting
3. join him
4. discuss
5. content
6. be sure to try

Option 2

1. daunting
2. looking at
3. follow him
4. take up
5. information
6. certainly consider

C Pragmatic Comprehension

01 Which advice was moderate? Which was strong?

02 What was the strongest piece of advice given in this dialogue? How do you know?

03 What do you think Troy will respond to Claire's last suggestion?

Grammar Brief ▶ p. 83

"Now that you've taken a bite would you like to know what it is?"

LESSON 08 / Proper Conduct   57

5 ATTENTIVE LISTENING

🎧 **Extended Dialogue** · *An office worker asks his co-workers about advice he has received.*

A Listen to the dining advice and write it below.

Should	Shouldn't

B With a partner, answer the questions below.

01 What does the man think about Claire's advice?

02 How does the woman feel about the boss? How do you know?

03 Why does the woman suggest not eating dessert?

04 What is the most important advice given?

❓ Are there any suggestions you disagree with? Why?

Audio Script — p. 89

QUOTE OF THE DAY

> What would Kierkegaard say about Socrates's advice? What would you say about it?

> Which advice are you more likely to use? Why?

"My advice to you is get married: if you find a good wife you'll be happy; if not, you'll become a philosopher."

— Socrates

"I see it all perfectly; there are two possible situations: one can either do this or that. My honest opinion and my friendly advice is this: do it or do not do it; you will regret both."

— Soren Kierkegaard

LESSON 08 / Proper Conduct

6 BUSINESS BASICS

A Are the behaviors below acceptable or rude to you while eating with someone?
Put a check next to the behavior you find acceptable. Compare your answers with a partner when you have finished.

	Behavior	You	Your partner
1.	belching	☐	☐
2.	chewing with your mouth open	☐	☐
3.	putting your purse/wallet on the table	☐	☐
4.	resting elbows on the table	☐	☐
5.	stacking dishes when you're finished	☐	☐
6.	slurping your drink or soup	☐	☐
7.	using utensils to gesture	☐	☐
8.	answering your phone	☐	☐
9.	texting on your phone	☐	☐
10.	eating before others at your table have been served	☐	☐
11.	blowing your nose at the table	☐	☐
12.	telling someone they have food stuck in their teeth	☐	☐
13.	picking up dropped utensils	☐	☐
14.	fix your hair	☐	☐
15.	your own:	☐	☐

B Group Think
In groups, discuss and answer the following questions.

› Look at items from the list in A; why you consider them rude or acceptable?
› Which of the above are you guilty of?
› What can you do as an alternative if you feel the need to do one one these?

LESSON 08 / Proper Conduct

7 TALKING SHOP

A Group Discussion
In groups, choose questions that interest you the most and discuss.

01 What's the best advice you've ever received or given?
02 Has etiquette changed in the past 20 years? If yes, how? If no, should it?
03 Are people too concerned about how others should behave? Why do you think so?
04 Which rule of etiquette really bothers you when people break it? How can you deal with someone who regularly breaks it around you?
05 What do you do if your boss has offensive manners? Have you ever been in this situation?
06 How do you tell someone you care about that their etiquette embarrasses you?
07 How would you react if someone told you you were doing something ill-mannered?
08 Your own: _____

8 DILEMMA

A deal you have been working on for weeks in Central Mexico is close to being finalized. After extended negotiations with your potential business partners, you were invited to eat a traditional delicacy for dinner. A positive impression at this meal could build the rapport you need to ultimately convince the partners to agree to terms. Having been to Mexican restaurants back home, you are familiar with Mexican cuisine and were looking forward to a memorable dinner.

Now at the restaurant, however, the food you have been served is much different than what you are used to. It looks similar to white beans, but it isn't. The waiter explains that the dish is "escamoles," or "ant larvae." One of your host corrects the waiter and states, "Actually, it's insect caviar, a savory delight once eaten by the Aztecs." He continues, "It's like a nutty, buttery, cottage cheese. Please enjoy." This host obviously places significant cultural value in sharing the dish with you and you don't want to offend him, but ant larvae is not what you had expected when you were told "traditional Mexican food."

TASK Decide whether you will you eat the dish or respectfully decline it. Explain what you will do, why you decided to do it, and what you will say.

After reading this chapter, I can...
... identify common Western etiquette practices
... use type 2 conditionals to give advice
... recognize and discuss acceptable manners while dining

SNEAK PEAK: > What was the last apology you made at work?

REVIEW 4

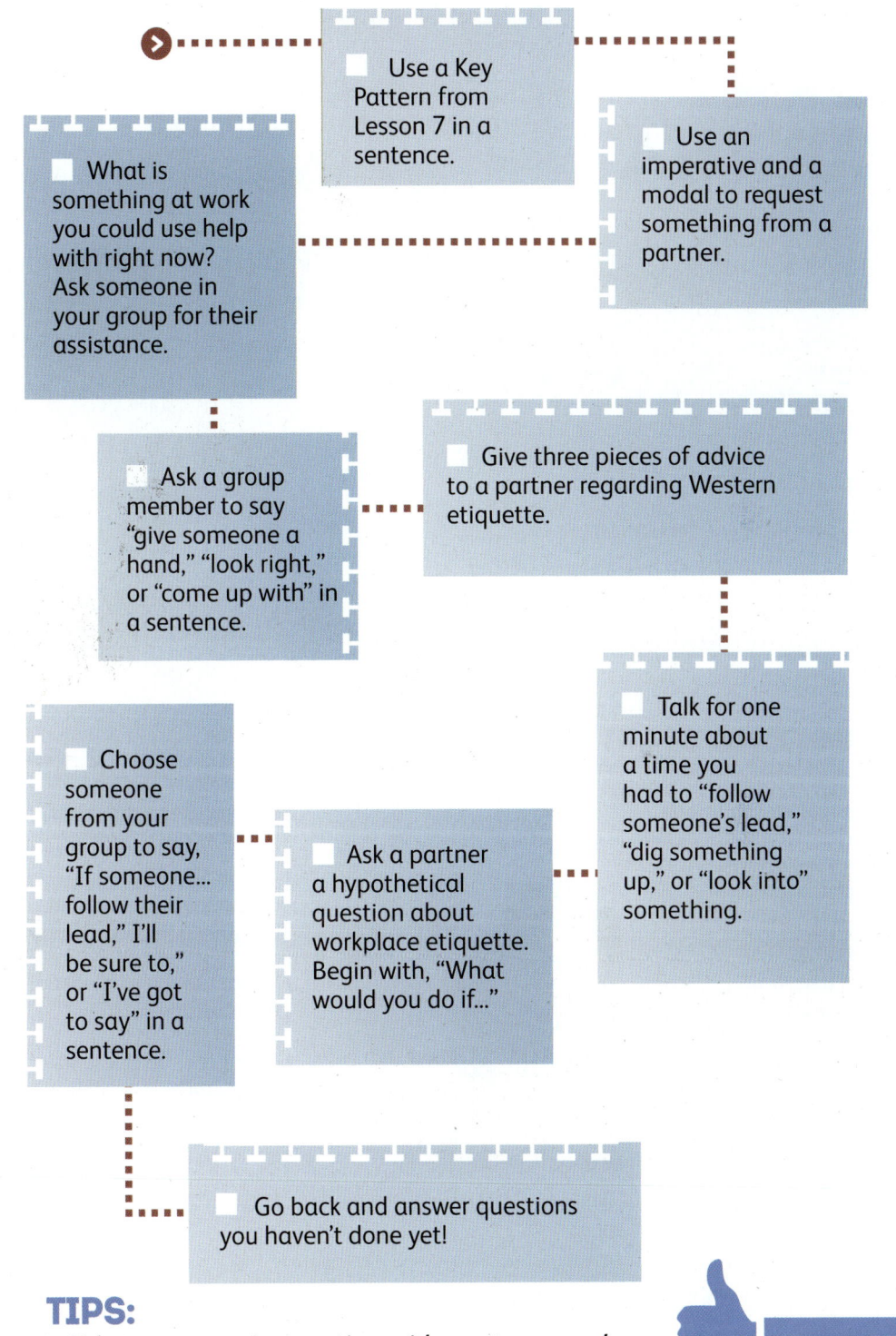

- Use a Key Pattern from Lesson 7 in a sentence.
- Use an imperative and a modal to request something from a partner.
- What is something at work you could use help with right now? Ask someone in your group for their assistance.
- Ask a group member to say "give someone a hand," "look right," or "come up with" in a sentence.
- Give three pieces of advice to a partner regarding Western etiquette.
- Talk for one minute about a time you had to "follow someone's lead," "dig something up," or "look into" something.
- Choose someone from your group to say, "If someone... follow their lead," "I'll be sure to," or "I've got to say" in a sentence.
- Ask a partner a hypothetical question about workplace etiquette. Begin with, "What would you do if…"
- Go back and answer questions you haven't done yet!

TIPS:
- Take turns answering questions with your team members.
- When you reach the end, go back and answer questions you haven't answered.

ALL DONE!

LESSON 09
SORRY FOR THAT

OBJECTIVES

After this chapter, you will be able to...

- apologize for causing an inconvenience
- use sequence words to organize your ideas
- assess apologies for effectiveness

1 GETTING STARTED

A Let's look at the image.
Describe what's happening in the picture.

What body language helps communicate apologies?

B Discuss the questions below:

› What might cause someone to get mad at another person's apology?

› What are the elements of an effective apology?

› What are the elements of an ineffective apology?

GOOD TO KNOW
Common Mistakes

Which is right? *Check the answers in the back of the book.*

› It's my fault. I really need to apologize **for / to** Jane.
› Susan can't make it today, so I must apologize **for / to** her.
› I'm sorry **for / to** your loss.

2 LANGUAGE PREVIEW

A Business Expressions
Read the following expressions and write your own sentence for each.

get on something: do something before it's too late.

E.g.) If you really want the position, you'd better get on it quickly and let them know you're interested.

Make your own: _____

be off by something: miscalculate or be wrong by an amount.

E.g.) When she asked how old I thought she was, I said thirty-five. I was off by four years!

Make your own: _____

run something by someone: show someone something for confirmation.

E.g.) Do you have a moment? I'd like to run my resume by you before officially applying.

Make your own: _____

B Key Patterns
Here are some key patterns that you can use when discussing a problem or solution.

I could use your help with...	It looks like I...	He's great with...
... making an apology	... made a mistake	... finding solutions
... getting this done	... might be late	... apologizing effectively
... some advice	... have to leave early	... crunching numbers

3 THE FORMAL SORT

A Formal or Informal?
With a partner, sort the expressions and explain why you believe it is formal or informal.

Please accept my apologies for...   Sorry for...   I take full responsibility.
It's my fault.   We have taken measures to...   We're going to...

Formal	Informal

4 INTERACTIONS

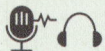 **A** Listen and fill in the blanks.

B Practice the dialogue with the options below.

A Big Mistake

Brooke: I could use your help with something. (1)_____ I sent the wrong quote to a client.

Bryce: (2)_____. Just get on it before it becomes an issue.

Brooke: That's the (3)_____. They already placed a rush order.

Bryce: How big was the order?

Brooke: Over $500,000.

Bryce: What were you off by?

Brooke: A zero. It should have been $5,000,000.

Bryce: What? Okay, tell them (4)_____. Include an apology and hope they understand.

Brooke: What should I say?

Bryce: Just tell them the truth. Before you do, (5)_____ Charles first. He's great with apologies.

Option 1

1. It looks like
2. No big deal
3. problem
4. as soon as possible
5. show it to

Option 2

1. Sadly
2. Don't worry too much
3. tricky part
4. as soon as you can
5. talk to

C Pragmatic Comprehension

01 What was Brooke's mistake?

02 Was Bryce concerned about Brooke's mistake? How do you know?

03 Does Bryce think Brooke should be careful? How do you know?

Grammar Brief ▶ p. 84

5 ATTENTIVE LISTENING

🎧 **Extended Dialogue** · *An office worker brings a draft apology to his co-worker for advice.*

A **Active Listening.** Think about the following questions as you listen. Write the answers in the spaces below.

> What does the woman want to know?

> What is the man's method of forming an apology?

> Which words help show the sequence of actions?

B **True or False.** *Circle T for true and F for false. Explain your answer.*

01 The man suggests saying, "I'm sorry if this caused any trouble."   T (F)   *"False! The woman asks why he thinks it's wrong."*

02 The man thinks Brooke's mistake wasn't significant.   T / F

03 The woman will take responsibility for the confusing error.   T / F

04 The man advises Brooke to have future quotes made by a senior associate.   T / F

05 The man is unclear with his advice.   T / F

 What do you think would be the best way to give this apology? Face-to-face? E-mail? Using SNS? Over the phone? In person? Another way?

Audio Script ▶ p. 90

QUOTE OF THE DAY

"You don't want to have to come into work on Monday already apologizing. I try to save my apologies for what I've done later in the week."

Ike Barinholtz

"I've made apologies to people I needed to, but I can't apologize to people I don't know for things they don't understand."

Sienna Miller

> What's your strategy for apologizing? Is there a time/place/person that you do or do not consider for apologies?

> What example from your life relates to one of the quotes above?

LESSON 09 / Sorry For That

6 BUSINESS BASICS

Corporate Apologies

A Effective or Ineffective?
Read the corporate apologies and choose whether they are effective or ineffective.

Software Developer Inc. @softdvlpr · 2 min
Our app tried 2 show the humorous lengths guys go 2 pick up women. We apologize if it's in bad taste & appreciate your feedback. #companyfail

Open ↩ Reply ⇄ Retweet ★ Favourite ··· More

Social Media: ☐ Effective ☐ Ineffective

"We're sorry for the massive disruption the oil spill caused people's lives. There's no one who wants this over more than I do. I'd like my life back."

We strive to make world-class products that deliver the best experience possible to our customers. With the launch of our new Maps last week, we fell short on this commitment. We are extremely sorry for the frustration this has caused our customers and we are doing everything we can to make Maps better.

Response to Reporter:
☐ Effective
☐ Ineffective

Effective Apology Checklist
› Acknowledge the problem
› Take responsibility
› Apologize directly
› Explain how you will prevent future problems
› Use an appropriate medium

Press Release:
☐ Effective ☐ Ineffective

B Pair work.
What was the problem with the ineffective apologies? Choose one ineffective apology and discuss what it needs to be effective. Rewrite it below.

....

....

....

....

....

LESSON 09 / Sorry For That

7 TALKING SHOP

A Group Discussion
In groups, choose questions that interest you the most and discuss.

01 What's the difference between an apology and an excuse?

02 Should you ever touch someone when apologizing? Why?

03 Are people too apologetic these days? Why?

04 Are you a forgiving person? What should you do when someone keeps making the same mistake?

05 When is it appropriate to apologize through e-mail, social media, or the telephone?

06 What's more important: an apology or never making the mistake again? Why?

07 When do apologies make you feel awkward? Give an example from your life.

08 Your own: ....

8 CASE STUDY

Below is a formal letter of complaint issued by an unsatisfied customer to Divan Hardware Store: "On June 11th I purchased a lawn mower in your store, but on June 20th it failed to start. I returned to the store to exchange the broken item. a salesperson told me that I came past the return date. He added that the store policy states that clients should contact the manufacturer for repairs. I tried explaining that it was impossible for me to go through a long negotiation process with the manufacturer. Instead of helping, the salesperson was very rude and refused to assist me. This is unacceptable and I will never shop at Divan's again."

Management recommendations:

01 The employee should take responsibility and apologize to the client. He should tell the customer he is greatly valued and invite the customer back.

02 The manager should call the customer and take responsibility. He should offer the service that was requested and explain that the employee's actions did not accurately reflect Divan's customer service policy.

03 The manager should apologize and take responsibility. He should offer what the customer initially requested, and explain that the employee acted in a way that represented store policy, but that the policy will subsequently be amended.

TASK Decide which of the three recommendations would you follow to resolve this conflict and explain why.

After reading this chapter, I can...
... apologize for causing an inconvenience
... use sequence words to organize your ideas
... assess apologies for effectiveness

SNEAK PEAK: > When is saying goodbye difficult?

LESSON 10
SAYING GOODBYE

OBJECTIVES

After this chapter, you will be able to...

- say goodbye after a business trip
- use passive tense to communicate your thoughts about people and accomplishments
- send a farewell e-mail to a colleague

1 GETTING STARTED

A Let's look at the image.
Describe what's happening in the picture.

What expressions are appropriate here?

B Discuss the questions below:

› What are good things to say when bidding farewell?

› How would you say goodbye to a close co-worker? What about a co-worker you weren't close to?

› How would your goodbyes change if you thought you weren't going to see the person again?

GOOD TO KNOW
Common Mistakes

Which is right? *Check the answers in the back of the book.*

› I'll definitely retire **by/ until** sixty years old.
› We'll probably go there **by/ until** 6 pm.
› I'll eat this pie **by/ until** tomorrow.

2 LANGUAGE PREVIEW

A Business Expressions
Read the following expressions and write your own sentence for each.

greener pastures: better conditions or opportunities.

E.g.) If you're going to quit your job, make sure you're leaving for greener pastures.

Make your own: ....

cross paths: meet someone in the future.

E.g.) We might be saying goodbye, but I hope we cross paths again someday.

Make your own: ....

keep in touch: maintain communication.

E.g.) It has been great meeting you. Please keep in touch even after you go.

Make your own: ....

B Key Patterns
Here are some key patterns that you can use when saying goodbye.

If you're ever... let me know.	I genuinely appreciate...	Give my best to...
... around...	... what you did	... your staff
... in the area again...	... your efforts	... the rest of the team
... back this way...	... your contributions	... your family

3 THE FORMAL SORT

A Formal or Informal?
With a partner, sort the expressions and explain why you believe it is formal or informal.

You were instrumental in...   You really helped with...   You will be missed.
I'll miss having you around.   Good luck in the future.   Best of luck in your future endeavors.

Formal	Informal

LESSON 10 / Saying Goodbye

4 INTERACTIONS

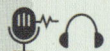 **A** Listen and fill in the blanks.

B Practice the dialogue with the options below.

Goodbye

Kim: So you came to say (1) _____ .

Cam: Yeah, it's (2) _____ .

Kim: I just want you to know how much we (3) _____ having you here.

Cam: Please, the pleasure was mine.

Kim: No really. You helped negotiate an important partnership and I (4) _____ appreciate your efforts.

Cam: Well thank you for (5) _____ .

Kim: If you're ever in the area again, please let me know.

Cam: I'll be sure to do that. The same goes for you.

Kim: Absolutely. Let's keep in touch on SynkedIn.

Cam: Definitely. Give my best to the rest of the (6) _____ . Sorry I couldn't say goodbye to everyone!

Option 1

1. farewell
2. time to go
3. valued
4. sincerely
5. saying that
6. staff

Option 2

1. so long
2. time
3. treasured
4. truly
5. the kind words
6. group

C Pragmatic Comprehension

01 Will Kim miss Cam? What makes you say so?

02 What expressions tell you Kim valued Cam's time?

03 How can you tell if Cam is leaving with positive feelings?

"He was a good boss, and we'll miss him... go ahead and kick his briefcase down, too."

Grammar Brief ▶ p. 85

5 ATTENTIVE LISTENING

🎧 **Extended Dialogue** · An office worker bumps into a colleague on his last day at the office.

A Listening Comprehension. *Listen and complete the questions below.*

› Do the colleagues have a close working relationship? How do you know?

› Does the woman respect her male co-worker? How can you tell?

› Do you think these workers will try and contact each other after this? Why?

B Matching
Match the utterances to the appropriate responses. With a partner to think of an alternative way of responding to the original utterance.

› I heard you're leaving.   Here's hoping.
› You're sticking around?   Yeah, it's time to move on.
› To greener pastures.   I'm a lifer.
› Maybe our paths will cross.   It's a nice work environment
› This is where I belong.   We'll see.

  What expressions would have made this farewell more personal or warm?

Audio Script   p. 90

QUOTE OF THE DAY

"Absence makes the heart grow fonder."

Aphorism

"Out of sight, out of mind."

Aphorism

› **In what situations are the above statements true?**

› **Which one applies most to business environments? Why do you think so?**

LESSON 10 / Saying Goodbye   71

6 BUSINESS BASICS

A Saying Farewell
A colleague is leaving and has sent you a farewell message. Read it and reply below.

↶ Reply   🗑 Trash   ▾ More   ◂ Previous   Next ▸

Tim R.
28th August 2014   19:17

Dear Jane,
This is just a quick message to let you know that Friday is my last day. I might not get a chance to see you before I go, so I wanted to say thank you for all of your help and support; I will always appreciate it. I'll miss having coffee with you! Please let me know if I can ever be of service to you. You can contact me on SynkedIn or via e-mail.
All the best,
Tim

Reply

LESSON 10 / Saying Goodbye

7 TALKING SHOP

A Group Discussion
In groups, choose questions that interest you the most and discuss.

01 Including body language, what ways do you know to say goodbye?

02 What is the best way to say farewell? Is that what you usually do? Why?

03 Which do you prefer: the excitement of new opportunities or staying with what you know? Why?

04 What causes an awkward farewell? Provide an example from your life if possible.

05 For politeness, is it important to say goodbye to people you don't like? What do you do in this case?

06 When was the last time you had an emotional goodbye? What made it so touching?

07 How do you ensure you keep in touch with someone you truly value?

08 Your own: _____

8 CASE STUDY

Anthony Chan is a young student who is completing an eight-month internship at the Summer Enrichment Program provided by Green Investors Group. As an intern he was able to work on annual reports and strategic plans, spend time at different departments and assist managers on various projects. His responsibilities included budgeting, assisting with accounts, and preparing various documents for review. Before leaving, Anthony would like to thank his two managers and co-workers in a professional manner.

The HR manager who hired Anthony and gave him this professional opportunity did not work with Anthony directly during these eight months. His direct supervisor was mostly in charge of the overall working process. The most directly useful people to Anthony have been experienced colleagues who mentored him.

Anthony wants to make sure that he expresses his gratitude for all the help he has received. He read in Forbes Magazine that thank you letters should be done promptly and by hand, but he is short on time and hand-writing is not his forte. As an alternative, he is thinking about writing a global thank you letter to everyone in the department, but give small tokens of gratitude to the two managers and a colleague.

TASK Decide (1) whether Anthony should thank everyone who has helped him or just those who have been the most helpful, and (2) whether he should write letters or thank them in person. Explain your decision.

After reading this chapter, I can...
... say goodbye after a business trip
... use passive tense to communicate your thoughts about people and accomplishments
... send a farewell e-mail to a colleague

SNEAK PEAK: > What do you do to welcome visitors from out of town?

LESSON 10 / Saying Goodbye

REVIEW 5

- [ ] Give an example of one good and one bad apology.
- [ ] What was the last mistake you made at work? How would you apologize for it in English?
- [ ] Talk about a sutation you "got on" before it became a problem. What did you do to prevent the problem?
- [ ] Tell each member of your group something you have appreciated about them or class.
- [ ] Talk with your group about when you'd use: "I could use your help with," "It looks like" and "he/she's great with" in a conversation.
- [ ] What have you learned in class? Make at least one passive and active sentence based on your experience.
- [ ] Use "greener pastures," "cross paths," and "keep in touch" to say goodbye to people in your group.
- [ ] Get a group member to use each of the following patterns: "If you're ever... let me know," "I genuinely appreciate," and "give my best to."
- [ ] You're done! Get up and have an open discussion with your classmates!

TIPS:
- Take turns answering questions with your team members.
- When you reach the end, go back and answer questions you haven't answered.

- [ ] **ALL DONE!**

Index

GRAMMAR BRIEF
76

AUDIO SCRIPTS
86

COMMON MISTAKES
(ANSWER KEY)
91

THE FORMAL SORT
(ANSWER KEY)
95

GRAMMAR BRIEF : APPENDIX
CONJUNCTIONS

A | Formation

(both) X and Y

means that X is true and Y is true. If X and Y are verbs, the assumption is that the events happened in the order they are mentioned.

I parked my car and went into the office. ≠ I went into the office and parked my car.

not only X but also Y

same as "X and Y" with the added implication that Y is somehow surprising or impressive.

He can speak not only Korean and English, but also German!

X or Y

could mean that only X is true, only Y is true, or both X and Y are true.

Someone should call the supplier, or write an e-mail, to find out when the shipment will arrive. (But both calling and e-mailing is OK.)

either X or (else) Y

means only X is true, or only Y is true. Never means both are true.

We should either extend the deadline, or cancel the project. (But not both)

neither X nor Y

means that X is false and Y is false. This is the opposite of "and," not the opposite of "or."

These product features are neither useful nor necessary. We should remove them.

B | Use

1. Make sure you are always join things of the same category

Two noun phrases
The break room and the staff meeting room are both on the second floor.

Two sentences
Either we sell at a 10% loss now, or we wait for another 6 months.

Two adjectives
This product is not only cheap, but also environmentally-friendly!

2. Singular-plural agreement

If you join subjects, they are usually treated as a plural subject, so make sure that verbs and pronouns agree properly :

Both the president and the vice-president are inspecting the office today.

A new laptop and a new tablet were needed for this project.

C | Practice

1: Select an appropriate conjunction, and make sure that verb agreement is correct.

All staff must attend at least one day of extra training on Thursday _____ Friday. We are discussing _____ the budget, _____ a new HR policy. Coffee _____ tea (*is/are*) available. A notebook _____ a laptop (*is/are*) useful for taking notes. Unfortunately, _____ the big conference room _____ the ballroom (*was/were*) available so we will meet in the small conference room _____ perhaps in the main hall.

2. Rewrite the passage with appropriate conjunctions.

Tim has a job. Jan has a job too. Tim works hard. He also has a good attitude. Jan doesn't work hard. She also doesn't have a good attitude towards her job. When she isn't sad, she is tired. If I had a choice between hiring Tim and Jan, there's no doubt who I would choose.

Both Tim and Jan have jobs.
_____
_____
_____

GRAMMAR BRIEF : APPENDIX
TIME

A | Formation

In spoken North American English, it is common to hear time told with the minute first.
With the minute first, use the expressions *past* or *after* (+ the current hour) if the minute is between the minutes 1-29. Use *to* (+the next hour) if the minute is between 31-59.

Between the minutes 1-29

[minute] + after/ past + [current hour]

Between the minutes 31-59

[minute] + to + [next hour]

When the minute is exactly 30

half past + [current hour]

Time Vocabulary

around	when the minute is within four minutes before or after the hour.
midnight	12:00 a.m.
noon	12:00 p.m.
quarter	when the minute is exactly fifteen before or after the hour.
sharp	at exactly the time (typically the hour).

B | Use

1. Minutes in the first half of the clock are past or after the hour.

  2:11 pm = 11 past 2
  2:11 pm = 11 after 2

2. After 30 minutes, count down to the next hour.

  4:50 = 10 to 5
  - *incorrect.* 50 after 4
  - *incorrect.* 10 before 5

3. When it is 15 minutes past, say it's "quarter after" or "quarter past."

  11:15 = quarter after 11
  11:15 = quarter past 11

4. When it is 15 minutes to the hour, say it's "quarter to."

  11:45 = quarter to 12

5. After exactly 30 minutes, say "half past."

  12:30 = half past 12
  - *incorrect.* 30 past
  - *incorrect.* 30 after
  - *incorrect.* 30 to

C | Practice

1. Write the given time in both hour first and minute first forms.

1:10 p.m.	It's one ten.	It's ten after one.
2:15 p.m.		
9:50 a.m.		
10:30 a.m.		
8:45 p.m.		

2. Convert the hour first time into minute first.

It's three oh five.	It's five past three.
It's ten fifteen.	
It's seven o'clock.	
It's four forty-five.	
It's six fifty.	

GRAMMAR BRIEF : APPENDIX
PREPOSITIONAL PHRASES

A | Formation

Prepositional phrases provide orientation when giving directions. Here is a helpful list to remember for giving directions : *across from, around the corner, between, beside, next to, down the hall, in, in front of, behind, on,* and *past.*

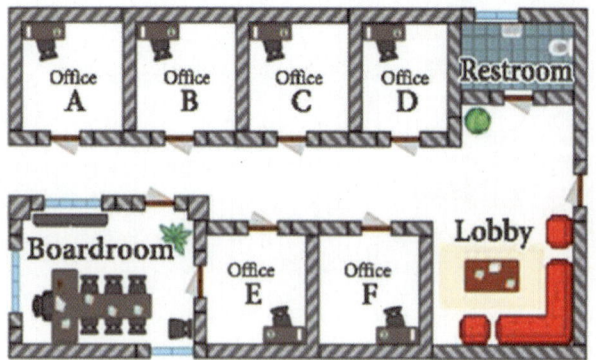

Example Use
- Office F is *across from* Office D.
- A plant is *around the corner* from Office A.
- Office B is *between* Office A and Office C.
- Office A and Office B are *beside* each other.
- The lobby is *down* the *hall* from the boardroom.
- A table is *in* the lobby.
- A chair is *in front of* the boardroom window.
- A chair is *behind* the lobby table.
- Papers are *on* the lobby table.
- Walk *past* Office A to get to Office B.

B | Practice

1. Fill in the blanks with the words in the box below.
   Use the office layout from Part A for reference. Answer the questions when you are done.

between	~~in front~~	on	down the hall	around the corner

e.g. - What's __in front__ of Office C?   *Office E and Office F*

- What's _____ from Office A and the boardroom?
- What's _____ the lobby and the boardroom?
- What room is _____ from Office D?
- What's _____ the boardroom desk?

2. Fill in the missing prepositions or prepositional phrases to complete the story.

I work in a nice little office on Main Street. I'm new, so mine's the smallest office there. The restroom is right _____ so everyone walks _____ my office to get to it. And it's also _____ from the lobby, so sometimes it gets noisy. If you walk _____, you'll pass all the offices. There's a boardroom at the end with a large window, but you can't see anything because there's a bookcase _____ it. I still don't know what's _____ there! I guess it's not much, but I'm happy with it.

GRAMMAR BRIEF : APPENDIX
DUMMY SUBJECTS

A | Formation

Simple Past Conversion

[subject] + [simple past]

* **There was a/an [noun] + [prep] + [noun]**

Sales rose. ▸ There was a rise in sales.
Sales dropped. ▸ There was a drop in sales.

Note *This is a simplified formula.*

Present Perfect Conversion

[subject] + [present perfect]

* **There has been a/an [noun] + [prep] + [noun]**

Sales have risen. ▸ There has been a rise in sales.
Sales have dropped. ▸ There has been a drop in sales.

Trend Vocabulary

	Verb Form	Noun Form
↑	rise / increase (in, of, to)	a rise / an increase (in, of, to)
↓	fall / decrease (in, of, to)	a fall / a decrease (in, of, to)
→	stay constant / remain steady / level out (at, around)	a leveling out (at, around)
~	fluctuate (between, around)	a fluctuation (between, around)

B | Use

In English all sentences need a subject. When the subject is empty, a dummy subject is inserted. In this section, "there" is the dummy subject.

Use dummy subjects for :

1) Stating trends.
There has been a drop in sick hours taken this year.

2) Identifying quantities.
There are thirty people in my office.

3) Explaining the presence of something.
There was a meeting at 10:00 a.m. this morning. Where were you?

C | Practice

1. Convert the sentences with subjects into sentences with dummy verbs.

Sales have dropped.	*There has been a drop in sales.*
The demand fell.	
Interest rose.	
The rate leveled out.	
Stock prices have fluctuated between $9-10.	

2. Convert the sentences with dummy verbs into sentences with subjects.

There was a fall in applications.	*Applications fell.*
There has been a decrease in sales.	
There was a rise in membership.	
There was a leveling out of prices.	
There was a fluctuation around $20.	

GRAMMAR BRIEF : APPENDIX
PRESENT PERFECT CONTINUOUS

A | Formation

Use **have** in the simple present, followed by **been** (*be* in the perfect), followed by the main verb with the **-ing** suffix.
We *travel*. → We *have been traveling*.

B | Uses

1) Event that started in the past, with effects that continue into the present.
- Our stock prices **have been increasing** steadily since 2012.
- I am exhausted because I **have been working** late every night this week.
- Kim **has been improving** her English by taking weekly lessons.

2) Expressing desires.
- I **have been wanting** a coffee all morning. (I started wanting it earlier, and I still want it now.)
- I **have been waiting** all week for this package to arrive. (I expected it Monday, it's still not here Friday.)
- The employees **have been hoping** for a raise. (They wanted one last year, they still want one this year.)

3) Specific lengths of time.
- That file **has been downloading** for 20 minutes. (And it's still not done.)
- We **have been meeting** regularly with the shareholders for a year now. (And we plan to continue.)

4) In a question, this tense often implies the speaker thinks the answer is 'yes'.
- **Have** you **been working out**? (I think you have, you look really healthy.)
- **Have** you **been reading** my e-mails? (I am accusing you of this.)

C | Practice

Practice the following dialogues with a partner. Choose between the simple present, present perfect, and present perfect continuous to correctly say each line.

A : (**you, see**) Sally?
B : (**she, rush**) around the office. (**she, get**) stressed out near deadlines.
A : (**I, try**) to get her attention all morning.
B : (**she check**) her e-mail regularly. Send her a message that way.

A : (**I, die**) for a coffee all morning.
B : (**you, leave**) for one right now? (**I, want**) a coffee too.
A : (**you, take**) cream or sugar?
B : (**I, cut back**) on those in the last year. (**I, drink**) coffee black these days.

A : Recently (**you, not meet**) standards for your ABC reports.
B : (**I, apologize**). (**I, not keep up**) with changes to the policy.
A : (**you, work**) for 10 years. (**we, expect**) better from you.
B : (**I, promise**) to follow the new format from now on.

GRAMMAR BRIEF : APPENDIX
PAST CONTINUOUS

A | Formation

Past continuous is formed by placing the past tense *was* (singular) or *were* (plural) in front of the main verb, and adding the suffix *-ing* to the main verb. There are no exceptions to this rule. (English continuous verbs are always exception-less).

B | Uses

1) To describe an action that was ongoing (not complete) at a particular time in the past.
- At 2:30 yesterday I **was busy writing up** the report.
- Thursday afternoon last week **we were tied up** in a board meeting.

2) It is useful for describing actions that were interrupted in the past. Use a phrase with past continuous to explain what happened, then a phrase with past simple explaining the interruption. Separate the two phrases with words like 'when' or 'but'.
- I **was writing** an e-mail **when I lost** my internet connection.
- Mary **was copying** documents to her own disks **when investigators caught** her.

3) Parallel actions (actions occurring at the same time) in the past. Separate them with while.
- Susan **was printing** the title page **while** Alex **was editing** the final paragraphs.
- Some workers **were getting fired**, while others **were being promoted**.
- The meeting **was carrying** on in one room, **while** the sale **was happening** in another.

C | Practice

1. Fill in the blanks with the appropriate verb forms to complete the sentences.

I [prepare] _____ when the phone (ring) _____ . It was my supervisor. She said the CEO (drop by) _____ early while they (set up) _____ the conference room.

Steve (delivering) _____ a presentation when the projector (stop) _____ . He (wrap up) _____ when suddenly it (start) _____ again.

Amy (eat) _____ lunch while she (work) _____ on her files. She (write) _____ an e-mail when Bob (stop by) _____ with a question.

2. Put these phrases in the correct order with the correct tense, and connect with "while" or "when."

[the photocopier (die)]	[Tony (make copies)]
[we (chat) in break room]	[suddenly the fire alarm (sound)]
[the latest model (create)]	[Frank (work) in the lab]
[a solution to the problem (strike) me]	[I (ride) the train this morning]
[Sharon (interview) a candidate in Room 101]	[Michael (interview) a candidate in Room 305]

GRAMMAR BRIEF : APPENDIX
IMPERATIVES

A | Formation

Politeness Level

▲

Less Polite

Note :
The extreme poles are acceptable in certain situations, but less recommended in general.

More Polite

▼

Statements (declarative)

Imperative (subject omitted)
[base verb] – *Copy the report for me by 5.pm.*

Imperative with 'please'
Please + [base verb] – *Please copy the report for me by 5.p.m.*

Questions (interrogative)

Modal
[modal] + [subject] + [base verb]

 Can you copy the report for me by 5.p.m?
could *Could you copy the report for me by 5.p.m?*
would *Would you copy the report for me by 5.p.m?*

Modal with 'if clause'
If + [subject] + [simple past], [modal request]
If I asked, would you copy the report for me by 5.p.m?

B | Use

In addition to the politeness strategies in Part A, you can add the idea of possibility to your polite requests. These are "hedging" strategies.

Add "If possible" to request statements that are a burden or might not be possible.
If possible, please pick me up on your way to work tomorrow.

Add "be possible to" or "be able to" for question requests that are a burden or might not be possible.
Would it be possible to get that report in by tonight?
Would you be able to get a sandwich for me while you're at lunch?

C | Practice

1. Turn the imperative statement into a polite request. (More than one answer is possible.)

Print me a copy of the report.
Would it be possible to print me a copy of the report?

Explain the report again.

Come in to work this weekend.

2. Change the overly-polite request into an appropriate one.

Would it be all right if you came to work on time?
Come to work on time!

Jane, if I asked again would you please not forward irrelevant e-mails to me?

Could you possibly finish this report by the deadline this time?

82

GRAMMAR BRIEF : APPENDIX
TYPE 2 CONDITIONALS

A | Formation

Condition (if clause)

If [subject] + [were/simple past]

If I were you...
If they had better resumes...
If you ate better...

Consequence (main clause)

[subject] + would/could + [simple present tense]

...I'd call them right away.
...they would have an easier time finding a job.
...you'd be much healthier.

Note: See Pre Business Basics 1 for Type 1 and Type 3 Conditionals.

B | Use

Use type 2 conditionals for:

1) Talking about hypothetical situations that are impossible or unlikely to happen.
"If I had wings, I would fly to work."

Contrast type 2 conditionals with type 1 conditionals which are for possible or more likely situations :
"I'll be so happy if you get the job!"

2) Giving advice.
"If I were you, I wouldn't worry so much about that."

3) Complaining.
"If my husband weren't so lazy, he'd be an upper-level manager by now :"

4) Consequences of an imagined situation.
"My wife would kill me if I got laid off."

Combine the main clause of a type 2 conditional with the condition of a type 3 conditional* with to show how a past action affects the present.
"The company would be in much better shape if the credit crunch hadn't happened."

* Type 3 conditional : If {subject} + [past perfect] ... {subject} + would/could + have + [past participle].

C | Practice

1. Draw a line connecting each clause to its best match.

If I had another chance...	if you had more time.
We would be surprised...	I would drive you to work.
If I had a car...	they would have more options.
I would try to visit you...	if you weren't satisfied.
If they had more money to invest...	I'm sure I'd do better.

2. Fill in the blanks using words in the text box below (more than one answer is possible). Change the verbs as necessary. Answer the questions when you're done.

| win the lottery   get promoted   could remember   ~~have more power~~   have more vacation   aren't afraid |

- What could you do if you *had more power* in your company?   - I'd restructure my department.
- What would you do if you _____?
- What would you do if you _____ everything?
- How would you react if you _____ today?
- What would you do if you _____ time?
- What would you do if you _____ of anything?

83

GRAMMAR BRIEF : APPENDIX
SEQUENCE WORDS

A | Formation

Starting a sequence :

first	firstly
first of all	to begin with
to start out with	initially

Ending a sequence :

last	lastly
finally	last of all
in the end	eventually

Sequencing :

next	then
after this/that	afterward
following this/that	

Numeric sequences :

first	second
third	fourth
fifth...	

note : that 12th is "twelfth" not "twelvth"

B | Practice

1. Connect the following sentences using appropriate sequence words.

- _____ Gregory worked in Russia. _____ He moved to Korea. *(then, first)*

- _____ the policy was approved. _____ it was repealed. _____ it was re-instated. *(finally, initially, then)*

- _____ I worked in accounting. _____ I was in Finance. _____ I was moved to payroll. *(in the end, after that, to begin with)*

- _____ Richard was only part-time. He worked for a year _____ he was full-time. _____ He was promoted. *(to start out with, eventually, after that)*

2. Put the sentences in the correct order, and use appropriate numeric sequence words.

You can now edit your file. Click on "Edit File". Click "File > Open". Find your file and select it.

Get three people to approve it. Write a proposal for the policy. Send the policy to HR. Circulate the proposal.

Wait for your pass to arrive in your employee mailbox. Send your application to Employee Services. Put your pass in your car window. Fill out a Parking Pass application form.

3. You are showing a new employee around work. Add sequence words where appropriate.

"_____ you should register for an employee e-mail address. _____ you should get keys at the Main Office. _____ just ask the secretary, Kim. _____ she is helpful. _____ you get your keys, _____ I recommend you get a parking pass. _____ you will probably want to double-check your pay information"

GRAMMAR BRIEF : APPENDIX
ACTIVE VS. PASSIVE

A | Formation

Active

Accounting *received* the pay slips.
Subject *verb* object

Passive

The pay slips *were received* by accounting.
Subject *passive verb* by object

Four differences :

(1) The object of the active sentence becomes the subject of the passive version.
(2) The subject of the active sentence becomes an optional object in the passive preceded by the word *by*.
(3) The main verb changes to its perfect form *e.g.* the one used in the present perfect or past perfect
(4) There is an extra verb *be* before the main verb in the passive. This verb takes the same tense as the main verb from the active sentence. *e.g.* John **fired** Mary → Mary **was** fired, John **would have fired** Mary → Mary **would have been** fired.

B | Uses

1. Shift the emphasis to the person affected by an action, away from the one doing the action.

- Shirley **was promoted** by upper management.
  (It's more important that it happened to Shirley, and less important that it was upper management who is responsible.)

- The shareholders **have been angered** by the latest decision.
  (The decision itself is less important than the reaction that it got.)

2. When you don't know, or don't want to say, who did some action, omit the by object in this case.

- The files **were deleted** from the computer.
  (And I'm responsible, but don't want to admit it.)

- The wrong items **were shipped** to a few customers.
  (We don't know made this mistake.)

Careful! Make sure that the main verb agrees with the appropriate grammatical subject, not with the person doing the action :

The security guard watched the CCTV cameras.
The CCTV cameras were watched by the security guard.
* The CCTV cameras was watched by the security guard.

The subject of the passive sentence is cameras (plural), so the main verb must be were, even though it is the singular security guard that is doing the action of watching.

Careful! Don't confuse prepositional phrases with objects of a verb.
You can only make a passive if there is an object. For example "The secretary arrives early in the morning." cannot be made into a passive.

(Early in the morning is arrived by the secretary.) because early in the morning is not an object.

C | Practice

1. Fill in the blanks with an appropriate noun. Then, re-write the paragraph using all active sentences.

Nouns :	
senior staff	the regulatory board
a courier	a committee
the department head	our company

"Our license needed to be renewed [by _____], and a renewal application had be to submitted [by _____]. A draft was written [by _____], and then some additions were made [by _____]. This was given final approval [by _____], then shipped out [by _____]."

....
....
....
....

2. Change all of the verbs in bold into the passive form.

"Construction crews **are fixing** sidewalks near Parking Lot#1 this week. Safety codes **require** everyone to use Lot#2. This work **may generate** a lot of dust, and we **advise** employees to close their windows."

....
....
....
....

85

AUDIO SCRIPTS

Lesson.01

INTERACTIONS

Zoe : Looks like I'm not the only one who needs a 3:00 boost.
Theo : Just brewed a fresh pot. I either drink coffee or I take a power nap.
Zoe : Both sound good to me.
Theo : I don't believe we've met.
Zoe : I'm Zoe. I started in Acquisitions on Monday.
Theo : Nice to meet you. My name's Theo, and I started in Accounting before coffee breaks were invented.
Zoe : I can't even imagine.
Theo : Not only did we not have coffee, but we had to use these gadgets called calculators.
Zoe : Well, it was nice meeting you. Thanks for making the coffee.
Theo : Any time.

ATTENTIVE LISTENING

Zoe : That doesn't look like any fun.
Steve : Yeah, we're waiting for it to clear up before we go to our cars.
Dan : I was smart enough to bring an umbrella, and then leave it in my car.
Zoe : It's rained every day since I moved to Miami.
Dan : Welcome to South Florida.
Zoe : There are worse places to live, trust me. I'm Zoe, by the way.
Steve : Steve. I've seen you in some meetings, but haven't had the chance to introduce myself.
Dan : Hey, my name's Dan.
Zoe : Great to finally meet you.

Lesson.02

INTERACTIONS

Anne : I'm free anytime this week after work.
Allen : When do you usually get off?
Anne : Most days I'm off by five-ish.
Allen : After 5:00 pm is fine. Okay, well, Tuesday works best for me.
Anne : I have a meeting at four o'clock that should wrap up by half-past five at the latest.
Allen : Let's say quarter to six?
Anne : 5:45 it is. Do you mind meeting at the coffee shop on 8th Avenue?
Allen : That works for me.
Anne : I'll call you Tuesday morning to confirm.
Allen : Thanks, Anne.

ATTENTIVE LISTENING

Anne : Hey, Allen, my four o'clock was pushed back an hour, so I really need to move our meeting later in the evening.
Allen : Would you rather meet up on Wednesday instead?
Anne : I'm having dinner with a college friend at 8:00 sharp.
Allen : What time would you need to leave to be there by 8:00?
Anne : 10 to at the latest.
Allen : So 7:50? Not a problem. I'll be at the cafe around ten after five.
Anne : I'll leave at 5:00 on the dot.
Allen : Thanks, Anne. I'm really looking forward to meeting with you.
Anne : Sorry to cancel like this, but we are set in stone Wednesday at 5:10.
Allen : No worries. You're doing me a huge favor! Talk to you tomorrow.

Lesson.03

INTERACTIONS

John : Excuse me, could you tell me what room the staff meeting is in?
Reception : Sure, do you know where the copy room is?
John : No, sorry, I'm new here.
Reception : Ok, it's on the third floor. Take the elevator and go left as soon as you get off.
John : So it's right there?
Reception : Not quite, you'll have to walk past some workstations. It's the big office near the end of the hall.
John : I see. Which side is it on?
Reception : The only place to go is right. Don't worry, you can't miss it.
John : Great; so third floor, left, end of the hall.
Reception : That's right. Good luck!

ATTENTIVE LISTENING

Monica : Can I help you?
John : Isn't this the boardroom? I thought there was supposed to be a meeting here.
Monica : Ah, that got switched to the main conference room. I guess you didn't get the SMS.
John : Oh, I left my phone in the car. So how can I get to the conference room from here?
Monica : It's a little far. You might want to just catch them next time.
John : That's not an option. We're firming up some plans and I need to be there.
Monica : All right, you might just make it. Go to the second floor, take a right and walk down the hall. It's across the overpass.
John : You mean that passageway between the buildings?
Monica : That's the one. You pass right over the street. Take a left once you cross it. It's the... second door on your right.
John : So I cross the overpass and go right?
Monica : No, left. Just look for the breakroom after the overpass. The conference room is between the breakroom and HR, so if you hit HR, you've gone too far.
John : Got it, thanks!

Lesson.04

INTERACTIONS

Grant : As you can see by the blue line, annual sales took a big hit in 2010.
Grace : Sorry, I can't read that. What did they bottom out at?
Grant : $50,000. But then there was a gradual rise in sales that peaked at $400,000.
Grace : Since then they've more or less leveled off.
Grant : Exactly, but not for our competitors.
Grace : Is the red line R. Motors?
Grant : That's B. Automotives. R. Motors is the green line.
Grace : It looks like they're trending in different directions.
Grant : But we're staying the same.
Grace : Okay, so let's discuss how to keep up with B. Automotives.

ATTENTIVE LISTENING

Janet : How did the stock perform over the last year?
Grant : This graph shows us that it started out strong in January at $22 a share, but declined slowly over the first quarter.
Janet : So when did it bounce back?
Grant : Not for a while. It bottomed out in the second quarter and leveled off. Toward the end of the second quarter, the stock rose rapidly.
Janet : How was the second half of the year?
Grant : It fluctuated in the third quarter, but hit a peak of around $24 per share.
Janet : And since then?
Grant : Since then it's been pretty steady. Throughout the fourth quarter there hasn't been much fluctuation.
Janet : So should we invest?
Grant : That depends how much you're talking. If we want to invest anything significant, we'd better wait until the market cools and the price falls a bit.

AUDIO SCRIPTS

Lesson.05

INTERACTIONS

Ruth : Hey superstar, what's going on in here?
Mark : Hey! Nothing out of the ordinary. Just slaving away.
Ruth : I could really use a drink. I've been wanting to get out of here since lunch.
Mark : And I've been wanting to sleep since I got up, but here we are.
Ruth : You know, there's a way to solve this problem.
Mark : Retirement?
Ruth : Now you're talking. Most people in here have been secretly hoping for that merger with Genetix... and a nice severance package.
Mark : Keep dreaming and I'll keep working.
Ruth : All right, I'll let you get back. But let me know if you change your mind.
Mark : Will do. Thanks for stopping by.

ATTENTIVE LISTENING

Mark : You still want to get that drink?
Ruth : Absolutely.
Mark : Well, I need to blow off a little steam. Where did you have in mind?
Ruth : There's this place called Momo's I've been wanting to try.
Mark : Okay, count me in. I need to get my mind off work a bit.
Ruth : Nice. To be honest, I have a bit of an ulterior motive.
Mark : What's that?
Ruth : I've been wanting to open a bar for a while now. It's kind of my dream. Do you mind checking it out with me?
Mark : Wait, your dream is to open a bar? Are you quitting?
Ruth : No, it'll just be a side thing for now. I'm hoping I can do both.

Lesson.06

INTERACTIONS

Quinn : What happened?
Paige : I was updating my software when the screen froze.
Quinn : Did you try restarting it?
Paige : Yeah, restarting didn't help. I tried turning the power off and on. No luck.
Quinn : You're the second person today with that problem. I'll have a look.
Paige : Do you think you can fix it by the end of the day?
Quinn : I'll try, but I wouldn't get my hopes up. That's actually what I was working on when you came in.
Paige : Ugh. When it crashed, I was working on a presentation. It has all my files.
Quinn : You didn't save to the cloud?
Paige : That's what the update was for!
Quinn : Right...sorry. I'll do my best.
Paige : That's all I can ask. Here's my card; could you call me at this number when you're done?

ATTENTIVE LISTENING

Quinn : I was fixing Paige's computer when I found a bug in the new software.
Vicky : That's bad news.
Quinn : Four other people had the same issue.
Vicky : I'll let others know not to update their system.
Quinn : No need. I was already writing an e-mail about it when you came in.
Vicky : Great. Let's nip this in the bud before we have more problems.
Quinn : No kidding. I'll be working on Paige's laptop the rest of the day.
Vicky : Will you still be able to go to the other branch this week?
Quinn : Hopefully we won't have any more problems, and I can make it there tomorrow.
Vicky : I'll just send someone else.

Lesson.07

INTERACTIONS

Will : Would you mind helping me with something?
Liz : Sure, what's up?
Will : I need you to look at an e-mail for me. Does this look right to you?
Liz : Yeah, but you might want to change the valediction.
Will : The what?
Liz : Valediction. The closing words in your e-mail.
Will : Why? What's wrong with my "valediction?"
Liz : "I expect your reply" sounds bossy.
Will : I couldn't come up with anything else. What can I say instead?
Liz : Try, "I look forward to." It's a lot friendlier.

ATTENTIVE LISTENING

Will : Thanks for your help with that e-mail earlier.
Liz : No problem. Anytime.
Will : I hate to do this to you, but I have to ask.
Liz : Another e-mail?
Will : Sorry! Would you mind looking at another one for me?
Liz : Actually, I don't have a lot of time right now. But I think Ben's free. Why not try him?
Will : I don't know. I guess I'm not that close with him.
Liz : He's a great guy. If I were you, I'd definitely ask him.
Will : Just one more e-mail. Come on, it'll just take a minute.
Liz : I'd love to, but in all honesty, I need to check my own e-mails.

Lesson.08

INTERACTIONS

Troy : I've got to say, dinner with the CEO is a little scary. I don't even know what fork to use.
Claire : You don't have to. Just start from the outside and work your way in.
Troy : All right, I can do that. Let's keep the advice rolling.
Claire : Okay, avoid answering your phone, texting, or anything like that. In fact, just turn it off.
Troy : I'll be sure to do that. What about alcohol?
Claire : You should probably follow Mr. Thompson's lead. If he orders a drink, do the same. Join him.
Troy : That's great, but what do I even talk about with him?
Claire : The website has a lot of info on him. You could probably dig something up there.
Troy : I'll look into that, thanks.
Claire : And last but not least, you absolutely cannot eat with your mouth open!

ATTENTIVE LISTENING

Drew : If you ask me, you should never drink alcohol at a business meal.
Troy : I don't know, Claire thought it was okay if Mr. Thompson ordered a drink.
Drew : I see her point, but I wouldn't.
Reese : Agreed. You also should eat slowly; take small bites.
Drew : Just try to finish your meal at the same time as everyone.
Troy : No problem there. I tend to eat at everyone else's pace.
Reese : And never order dessert.
Troy : What?
Drew : She's kidding. No boss is that cruel.
Reese : The best advice for you is probably to relax and have a good time.

AUDIO SCRIPTS

Lesson.09

INTERACTIONS

Brooke : I could use your help with something. Unfortunately I sent the wrong quote to a client.
Bryce : It happens. Just get on it before it becomes an issue.
Brooke : That's the thing. They already placed a rush order.
Bryce : How big was the order?
Brooke : Over $500,000.
Bryce : What were you off by?
Brooke : A zero. It should have been $5,000,000.
Bryce : What? Okay, you need to tell them ASAP. Include an apology and hope they understand.
Brooke : What should I say?
Bryce : Just tell them the truth. Before you do, run it by Charles first. He's great with apologies.

ATTENTIVE LISTENING

Brooke : What's wrong with saying, "I'm sorry if this caused any trouble"?
Charles : First, you should be sorry regardless. Second, it did cause trouble; it was a major calculation error.
Brooke : OK, so what should I say?
Charles : Start by telling them the situation, like, "There was an error in the quote I sent. It was missing a zero."
Brooke : And then?
Charles : Next you need to acknowledge the damage it caused. So say something like, "I am truly sorry that this error caused you to place an order for the wrong amount."
Brooke : OK, how's this, "I mistyped the quote I sent you. I'm sorry that it has created confusion and caused you to make an order for the incorrect amount."
Charles : Right, so you're acknowledging the problem and taking responsibility. Finally, tell them how you'll correct the situation so it won't happen again.
Brooke : Any ideas for that?
Charles : Try, "From now on, we will have all quotes confirmed by a senior associate before sending them."

Lesson.10

INTERACTIONS

Kim : So you came to say goodbye.
Cam : Yeah, it's about that time.
Kim : I just want you to know how much we enjoyed having you here.
Cam : Please, the pleasure was mine.
Kim : No really. You helped negotiate an important partnership and I genuinely appreciate your efforts.
Cam : Well thank you for that.
Kim : If you're ever in the area again, please let me know.
Cam : I'll be sure to do that. The same goes for you.
Kim : Absolutely. Let's keep in touch on SynkedIn.
Cam : Definitely. Give my best to the rest of the team. Sorry I couldn't say goodbye to everyone!

ATTENTIVE LISTENING

Jill : I heard you're leaving us.
Cam : Yeah, I'm afraid it's time to move on.
Jill : To greener pastures no doubt.
Cam : Here's hoping. You're sticking around?
Jill : Yeah, I'm a lifer. I guess this is where I belong.
Cam : It's a nice work environment.
Jill : Well, uh, keep up the good work wherever you are. Maybe someday our paths will cross again.
Cam : Sure. We'll see.
Jill : Take care.
Cam : You too.

ANSWER KEY
COMMON MISTAKES

01

1 : I bought him a present. I did it **for** him.
2 : Apples are good **for** you.
3 : My co-worker is good **to** me.

1) do something for someone : the action is intended for the person's benefit
   - My kids are always doing little things for me like drawing pictures or writing notes.

2) do something to someone : the action is harmful
   - I have so much work that I barely sleep. I think my boss is doing this to me on purpose.

3) to me : in my opinion
   - To me, all dogs look alike.

4) be good to: treat someone well
   - My manager is very fair in the office. I think he's quite good to us.

5) be good for : beneficial
   - Meeting Sam has been good for my career. He has so many connections.

02

1 : Do you have **the** time?
2 : Thanks, I had **a** great time.
3 : There's **a** time for action, and **the** time is now.

1) the time : the time is a specific reference known by the speaker and listener. "Do you have the time?" means, "What time is it?" Without any context, the listener can assume the speaker means *now*.
   - Sorry, my cell phone just died. Do you have the time?

   Note : "Do you have a time?" is incorrect. Avoid confusing this for, "Do you have any time?" which asks if the listener is free to do something.

2) have a great time : enjoy yourself
   - You must have had a great time on your trip; these pictures look amazing!

03

1 : Of course I know how to get there. It's common **knowledge**!
2 : Not talking in an elevator is common **courtesy**.
3 : It's common **sense** that you shouldn't do business with a criminal.

1) common sense : no one needs to tell you; you should be able to tell by yourself
   - Not touching fire is just common sense.

2) common knowledge : most people in a group share this information
   - Yes, I know who the President of the United States is. It's common knowledge. (But not common sense).

3) common courtesy : courtesy that people in a group or culture share
   - Saying hello to your co-workers in the morning is common courtesy. People would look at me like a jerk if I just went straight to my office.

ANSWER KEY
COMMON MISTAKES

04

1 : **What** do you think about the market?
2 : **How** can you solve this problem?
3 : **How/What** do you know about that?

1) what do you think about something : what is your opinion about something
   - What do you think about Bitcoin? Do you think it will ever replace paper money?

2) how do/can you : what is the process involved
   - How do I think? Good question, but I'm not a neuroscientist!

> Note : How do/can you think about something indicates judgment in certain contexts.
> e.g. I'm talking to you about our deficit; how can you think about taking a vacation!

05

1 : Hi Bob, I'll see you **in ten minutes**.
2 : Jane and Michael will get married next year. **Nine months later** they'll have a baby.
3 : The meeting will finish **in twenty minutes** today.

1) later : compares two times. After you state a reference time, then later may be used. Later cannot be used with only one point in time.
   Correct This class finishes in two weeks. I'll go to the US a week later.
   Incorrect I'll go to the US three weeks later.

2) how do/can you : what is the process involved
   - How do I think? Good question, but I'm not a neuroscientist!

> Note : if no time is provided, it indicates an indefinite future time.
> e.g. I'm not sure when I'll have time, but I promise to get those documents to you later.

3) in [unit of time] : the point in time something will be happen
   - Traffic is going to get crazy soon, so let's leave in ten minutes or so.

06

1 : A | When will you go?   B | **I don't know**.
2 : A | It won't rain at all next month.   B | **I don't know about that**.
3 : A | Coffee was thrown out of your window.   B | Well, I **don't know about that**.

1) don't know
   (1) not have knowledge of something or be uncertain about it
   - I don't know if I will retire next year or not. I need to look carefully at my finances first.

   (2) disagree
   - You want to quit your job to become a dog walker? I don't know, that sounds extreme.

2) don't know about

   (1) to deny knowledge of something, especially after an accusation
   - I don't know anything about that missing paper. Go accuse someone else!

   (2) disagree with someone's conclusion
   - A : Shelly will probably quit soon.
   - B : I don't know about that. It seems like she's starting to actually enjoy it here.

07

1 : Need help? **What's wrong**?
2 : Why are you being so rude? **What's wrong with you**?
3 : You look upset. **What's wrong**?

1) what's wrong : what is the problem or trouble you are experiencing?
   - You don't seem like yourself. What's wrong?

2) what's wrong with you : you have a problem with you
   - You're really annoying today. What's wrong with you?

   Note : this expression is used in a judgmental tone and will likely cause offense.

08

1 : I like dog. (this means you like dog meat)
2 : Let's go restaurant. (this means you are cheering for the restaurant)
3 : Everyone ate some of the pate. It was a communism dish. (the dish supported communism)

1) non-count animal : the animal's meat
   - I don't like chicken very much. I prefer red meat.

2) countable animal : the animal
   - I really like chickens. They're so cute!

3) let's go [name]! : a cheer during a competition
   - I think we can win this game. Let's go, Yankees!

   *Note : English learners may say, "Let's go restaurant," when they mean, "Let's go **to a** restaurant." Let's go to a reastaurant indicates you would like to physically travel to the restaurant, opposed to cheering for it.*

4) communism : a political and economic system based on common ownership
   - Countries like Cuba and the former USSR have struggled under communism.

5) communal : shared
   - In some cultures, it is common to have a communal dish that everyone eats from at dinner.

ANSWER KEY
COMMON MISTAKES

09

1 : It's my fault. I really need to apologize **to** Jane.
2 : Susan can't make it today, so I must apologize **for** her absence.
3 : I'm sorry **for** your loss.

1) apologize to someone : the offender says they are sorry to the person who was offended
   - I apologized to my former boss after I got him fired.

2) apologize for someone : the offender is not willing or able to apologize to the offended person, so a third person apologizes in the offender's place.
   - I apologize for Jane. She's not usually like this. I guess she's had too much to drink.

3) sorry for : indicates genuine sympathy, often (but not always) responsibility
   - I'm truly sorry for your loss. If you need anything, I'm here for you.

3) sorry to [base verb] : indicates sympathy
   - Sorry to hear you lost your job. Here's hoping you get another soon.

   Note : a base verb is needed after **to**.

10

1 : I'll definitely retire **by** sixty years old.
2 : We'll probably be there **by/until** 6 p.m.
3 : I'll eat this pie **by** tomorrow.

1) by [time] : something will be done at the given time or before
   - I'll send the report by 5:00 p.m., maybe sooner!

   Note : with many verbs, by indicates completion.
   e.g. I'll eat the cake by lunchtime. It'll be gone by then.

2) until [time] : an action will continue up to the given time and then stop
   - 'll eat the cake until lunchtime. If I haven't finished it, it's going in the garbage.

ANSWER KEY
THE FORMAL SORT

> **Note** *formality and politeness are not always the same. In modern English, a polite, less formal register is typically used in business environments.*

Formal / More Formal	Less Formal / Informal
» No contractions	» Contractions
» Full sentences	» Ellipsis
» Avoid Idioms	» Idioms
» Modals : could, would, may, might	» Modals : can, will (in questions)
» Firm or direct regarding facts or figures	» Imprecise or indirect regarding facts or figures
» Longer words, Greek/Latin origins	» Shorter words, Germanic origin
» Noun form preferred over verb form (nominalization)	» Verb forms preferred over noun form
» Passive voice	» Active voice
» Euphemistic language	» Indelicate or inelegant language

Chapter	More Formal	Less Formal / Informal
1	• It's beneficial for… • I support… • …yet it may lead to…	• It's good for… • I'm for… • …but it's bad for…
2	• Do you have a moment? • When would you like? • At approximately five o'clock…	• Are you free? • When's good? • Around five-ish…
3	• Could you tell me where… • Certainly! Follow this hall… • Turn left…	• Do you know where… • Sure, just go… • Hang a left…
4	• There has been an increase in sales. • Stocks fell sharply. • Rates remained steady.	• Stocks are going up. • Stocks went down quickly. • Rates stayed the same.
5	• I aspire to… • It would be of benefit to… • My greatest desire is to…	• I hope to… • I wish I could… • My dream is to…
6	• The inconvenience was… • I attempted to… • Most assuredly…	• The problem was… • I tried to… • Of course…
7	• Would you mind… • No, not at all. • Unfortunately, there's no way I could…	• Can you… • Sure, what's up? • Sorry, I'm a little busy.
8	• To me, it's absolutely unacceptable to… • I have no issue with it. • As opposed to…, you should…	• You can't… • It's all right. • Instead of…, just…
9	• Please accept my apologies for… • I take full responsibility. • We have taken measures to…	• Sorry for… • It's my fault. • We're going to…
10	• You were instrumental in… • You will be missed. • Best of luck in your future endeavors.	• You really helped with… • I'll miss having you around. • Good luck in the future.